BE HAPPY

What makes you happy – really, truly happy?

Happiness can come from a thousand different things. For some it's spending time with friends, for others it's curling up on the sofa with a mug of hot chocolate and a good movie. Whatever it is that makes you happy, it's that deep feeling of joy and contentment that everyone is chasing, that wonderful warmth when you just have to smile.

That's why we, the editors of *Teen Breathe*, decided to put together this book. Every month we read piles of research about what it takes to feel fulfilled, and we've learned there are simple things everyone can do to make reaching that smiley state even easier. Now we're excited to pass that knowledge on to you.

So next time you find yourself in need of a boost, this book is here to offer a helping hand. Life isn't always easy and there will be times when obstacles may feel insurmountable. But we hope the following pages will remind you of all that's positive in your life. Because if you're happy with what you have, you will always have what you need.

SMILE AND BE HAPPY

CONTENTS

HAPPY TALK

What is happiness to you? For some it's being with their friends, enjoying a lie-in or getting that new box-set they've wanted for ages. For others it's about wellbeing – a feeling of physical and emotional contentment within. This is what most people want to experience: happiness that feels bone-deep, which comes from having a positive attitude, being fulfilled with their life and having good relationships. Let's look at five myths that surround happiness...

MYTH 1

You're born happy or you're not; it's not something you can change

It may surprise you to know that you have more influence over your happiness than you've probably given yourself credit for. Research has found that between 25 and 35 per cent of your potential for happiness is determined by your genes. So whether your parents are grumpy all the time or constantly smiling doesn't have a huge impact on how you feel. Equally, what school you go to, your age, gender and where you live only account for 10 to 15 per cent, which means that around 50 per cent of how happy you can be in your life is determined by you. How you view events, how you react to them and how you approach the world can all affect how happy you feel.

MYTH 2

Happiness is a goal to strive for and reach

Do you ever feel that if you achieve a certain award or buy a particular product, then you'll be happy? You can pursue a moment of happiness and experience it, but once that burst of pleasure is over you're back to how you felt before. Studies have shown that, although lottery winners experience an initial boost in happiness levels, within a year they return to their original level. True happiness doesn't come with rainbows and fireworks but instead stems from a calmer sense of contentment and lasting joy because it is an ongoing process that continues throughout a person's lifetime.

MYTH 3

To be happy you can never be sad

Everyone is sad and stressed sometimes. Everyone. Even the annoying person who seems to be the happiest person in the world. It's important to understand this emotion, too, because by knowing how sadness and difficulties feel, you can appreciate joy and contentment more. Experiencing sorrow and anguish and learning to overcome them with methods such as mindfulness, or practising gratitude for all the positivity in your life, will mean you are better able to cope with life's challenges.

MYTH 4

It's selfish to think about your own happiness

Lots of people have the view that focusing on your own happiness must mean you're selfish. If this was the only thing a person thought about then, maybe. However, happy people spread happiness. One idea – called the Three Degrees of Influence – suggests your positive, happy attitude and actions rub off not only on your friends, but also on their friends, and in turn, their friends. So make sure you look after yourself and next time you're feeling happy, let the world know. Remember, however, if you're stressed or in a bad mood, those around you can see or feel that mood, too.

MYTH 5

If I let myself be happy, something bad is bound to happen

Many people have experienced a moment when they are truly happy but then suddenly panic that it won't last and life will take a turn for the worse. Sadly, some also think that if they don't let themselves feel joyful that it will protect them from any hurt and pain that might come their way. This prevents them living life to the full because they spend too much time worrying about what could go wrong in the future to ruin their happiness. If this ever happens, consider all the things you have to be thankful for compared to whatever you're worrying about. It challenges fearful feelings while supporting the joy you're experiencing, and research shows practising gratitude increases and deepens the happiness you experience.

SMILE LIKE YOU MEAN IT

Did you know that your beautiful smile has amazing benefits for both you and the people around you? Discover how the simple act of smiling more can make the world a cheerier place

Smiling comes naturally when you're carefree and feeling good. It's easy to grin when life is going well – but how about the times when life is challenging, exhausting or just plain hard work?

The stresses and strains of responsibilities can make it more of a struggle to smile. The demands of homework, routine, chores, exams and expectations can take you out of the moment and make you lose touch with your bright, joyful self.

When this happens, you're more likely to scowl than grin, but your smile holds the key to a happier life. Look upon your facial expression as a kind of mood barometer. Are you wearing a fair-weather smile or a rainy-day frown? Though it may not feel like it, the choice is actually yours.

Of course, there will be days when you don't feel like smiling but do it anyway. Give yourself a big, toothy grin in the mirror. Smile so your eyes sparkle and notice how that feels. Things might not immediately change on the outside, but you can change how you feel on the inside right this moment and that makes all the difference to your self-esteem and sense of wellbeing.

DID YOU KNOW?

* Smiling enhances your mood. When you smile, feel-good neurotransmitters in your brain release dopamine, endorphins and serotonin, the natural chemicals that make you feel happy, relaxed and carefree.

* Whether you have good reason to be happy or not, the facial muscles you use to smile can trigger the release of endorphins, so the more you smile the better you feel.

* Smiling not only boosts happy endorphins, it also helps to reduce the stress hormone, cortisol, which means you'll feel less anxious and more at ease.

* As a result of those clever endorphins, smiling is an effective pain reliever. If you bruise your knee or knock your elbow, grin and laugh off the pain. It really does help.

* When you keep grinning through life's various challenges, remembering to wear a natural smile in a situation such as a job interview, it'll help you'll feel uplifted, relaxed, confident and more positive.

* The world-famous smiley face was created in 1963 by the artist Harvey Ball who understood the power of a smile. In 2001, the Harvey Ball World Smile Foundation was established in his honour, and a World Smile Day takes place each year. See worldsmileday.com.

* No matter where you go, you don't need an interpreter for smiles. Smiling can help you connect with people all over the world. It's the universal language of happiness.

* Grinning is attractive. It makes you appear warm, friendly and approachable. If you're looking to make new friends, build lasting relationships and share some happiness with the world around you, be more generous with your smiles.

WAYS TO BRING MORE SMILES INTO YOUR LIFE

* Have a smile party. Surround yourself with happy, positive-minded, fun-loving people and focus on enjoying life's light-hearted, joyful moments.

* Vow to be a smiley person and set out to gift a grin to all those you meet.

* Make time for self-care. It's easier to smile when you're making space in your life for what matters.

* Carry a smile totem with you – something that can't fail to put a smile on your face even when you've had a challenging day. Perhaps it's a cute animal picture, funny photo or a big smiley key ring.

* Make time to play. Have fun. Be present in the moment. Laugh lots and make grinning your go-to expression of choice.

Get your smile on…
Take a moment to think about the people, pets, spaces and places that help lift your frown and then make a note of them here. Keep your list in a safe place and reach for it when you're in need of inspiration.

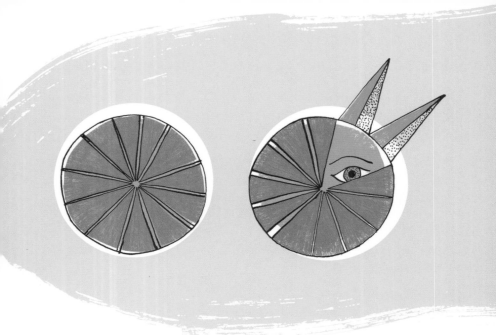

The secret to
HAPPINESS

Think about what would make you happy... a new pair of jeans, a smart tablet, a designer bracelet? Perhaps. But smiles raised by consumer items often fade quickly. Real happiness is something that comes from within – and it stands the test of time

Understanding happiness

Let's start by trying to define happiness. This is tricky because happiness is a personal thing. What makes you happy might prompt a bemused shrug of the shoulders from your peers. Past experiences, environment and relationships with family, friends and even teachers all contribute to how happiness is felt. Perhaps, however, the key lies in how long it lasts. The 'wow' effect from the purchase of a new phone tends to be a short, fleeting pleasure. It doesn't last. The inner contentment experienced when you feel fulfilled sticks around. It's what makes you smile for no real reason.

Happiness = heart + brain

If happiness is different for everyone, how can we all look for the same thing? Many people think happiness is found in the heart. 'My heart is going to burst!' and 'My heart is filled with joy!' are common exclamations of happiness. Yet the organ that's actually responsible for happiness is the brain. It releases chemicals that carry messages, some of these are happy, others are more sombre. The good news is that you can encourage your brain to keep sending more of the happy messages, much in the same way you might add a smiley emoji at the end of a WhatsApp. *Keep reading to find out how…*

The science behind happiness

This is where neuroscience (the science of the brain) comes in useful. There is still much we have to learn about the brain, but several studies are now exploring how it affects a person's wellbeing. Some are exploring if people are simply born happy (or not). In other words, does the answer to whether or not someone will be a happy person lie in their DNA – the complex chemical structure that carries their genetic information? The evidence suggests it might be a factor, there could be a genetic connection. But it's not the whole story. For while you can't change your DNA (for now, anyway), you *can* affect your environment and the way you react to it.

TRAIN YOUR BRAIN

Science has shown you can control your happiness by 'forcing yourself' to feel positive emotions. How? You create more positive experiences. There are several ways to do this:

1 Positive thinking
Repeating upbeat, optimistic phrases such as 'I will succeed', 'I'm not afraid', 'I am intelligent' and 'I am beautiful' can lead to more happy thoughts.

2 Mindfulness exercises
Practise being fully aware of your environment and the activity in which you are engaged. From mindful observation (noticing and appreciating the tiniest aspects of your environment, say, a raindrop splashing onto a window) to mindful immersion (paying close attention to an activity, be it drawing, reading, even cleaning your bedroom), focusing your thoughts in this way has been proven to lower stress and anxiety.

3 Gratitude
Keeping a gratitude diary where you say thank you for all the small things in life that make you happy can help to reduce negative emotions such as envy, frustration and regret.

4 Physical exercise
Team or individual, structured or unstructured, sport and general physical activity is shown to boost energy levels and improve your general sense of wellbeing. Outdoor pursuits are especially beneficial as natural light is scientifically proven to enhance your mood.

SO, WHAT MAKES YOU HAPPY?

What makes each person happy will depend on many factors, not least their genetics and environment. Contentment, however, could be described as a general inner sense of peace and fulfilment. There may be times when outside events make it more difficult to find – and you have to wait a while and work quite hard to get it back – but it will be there ready for you to pick up again. A happy life starts from within and sustained happiness isn't a short-term pleasure purchased online or in a clothes shop. So, what makes you truly happy – what really gives you a sense of inner peace and fulfilment?

Here are a few prompts that might help you to discover the people, places, times and things that make you happy. And remember, there are no right or wrong answers – it's a personal, subjective thing…

* Think of 10 things (big or small) that bring you an inner sense of happiness and contentment.

* Choose 10 words to describe how your happiness feels.

* Think of five people who make you smile.

* Think of five places you feel at home.

* Choose five favourite meals.

* Think of five activities and events you love.

* What are your five most treasured possessions?

* Think of five little things you do every day.

* What else could you do to feel happy?

CARRY ON LAUGHING

Tears streaming, stomach aching, heart lifting? If you're just recovering from a fit of the giggles, you'll have done yourself the world of good

Nothing beats the feeling of having a good giggle. Having a friend who shares your sense of humour is fun and a great way to connect. But why is this? Research suggests laughter releases the body's feel-good endorphins, which help people to feel relaxed and promote bonding.

It seems a shame then that while children laugh 300 times a day, for adults the figure is a miserly 20. Message? Hold onto those giggles – even when you're changing schools or sitting exams – and try not to let life get too serious.

And, anyway, laughter has a serious side. It's good for your mood and health. When you laugh, the amount of stress hormones in the body decrease, which helps to boost the immune system and prevent illness. One study even found that people with a good sense of humour live longer.

People laugh when they're having fun, but laughter can also happen when you're nervous and on edge, perhaps because of its healing, stress-relieving properties. Have you ever felt an uncontrollable urge to snigger when being scolded by a parent or teacher? You might laugh when you're nervous or embarrassed, which is also a regular, healthy response. Laughter with friends can get you through difficult days at school and take your attention away from the more challenging side of life. When you laugh, you're right there in the moment, letting go of the past and worries about the future.

ARE YOU LAUGHING?

Have you ever tried laughing for no reason? It may seem strange to laugh when nothing's funny, but what's interesting is that fake laughter has all the same health benefits as real laughter.

Dr Madan Kataria from Mumbai in India decided to test the theory. He started a laughter club where volunteers told jokes to get each other giggling. As time went on, however, the good jokes ran out and became more hurtful and cruel. That's when he developed the idea of laughter exercises – ways to generate laughter without telling jokes. He invented the concept of Laughter Yoga, which is now a worldwide movement. It's like a gift from a man who felt he didn't really have a good sense of humour. What he found was that by practising regular Laughter Yoga, he got in the laughter zone and it helped him to tell good jokes more naturally.

Do you know someone who brightens up your day, a friend, relative or teacher maybe, who always shifts people's mood by bringing in playfulness and giggles? Dr Kataria believes everyone can hone and develop this natural skill. To help you along, here are a few laughter exercises to get you started. You can practise them alone, but they're even more fun with a friend or as a group.

LAUGHTER EXERCISES

1 Smiling warm up
Laughter Yoga teacher Robert Rivest suggests this exercise: 'Take a slow, long, deep breath in and smile while saying to yourself: "As I breathe in, I smile." As you slowly breathe out, say: "As I breathe out, I release all physical tension."'

2 Laughter breathing
Take a long, slow, deep breath in and stretch your arms up in the air. As you lower your arms have a good belly giggle for as long as you can. Can you feel the way your belly moves when you have a good chuckle? That's the kind of deep laughter that massages the internal organs and has lots of health benefits.

3 Milkshake laughter
This is one of Dr Kataria's most popular exercises. Pretend you're mixing up a milkshake by pouring two imaginary containers of liquid into a glass. Now take a sip as you inhale, and exhale out laughter.

4 Mobile phone laughter
Hold an imaginary phone to your ear and pretend you're listening to a hilarious joke. You can also try this with your real phone and pretend you're having a giggly conversation with a friend. Maybe you could even try it walking down the street.

5 Mexican wave laughter
This one is great for groups. Line up and do a Mexican wave, where each person in turn lifts their arms in the air to make a wave shape. Start with your arms hanging down towards the floor to get a good wave effect as you raise them high above your head and then keep laughing as each person in the group follows suit.

ATTITUDE OF GRATITUDE

How often do you stop and think about all the everyday things you're thankful for? Getting into the habit of noticing these things can shape the way you see the world

Recent studies show that developing an attitude of gratitude can help people to become happier, more optimistic and relaxed, as well as more resilient when things don't work out the way they'd anticipated.

The words 'think positively' are bandied about a lot, but the idea – that by doing so you're more likely to act and feel positive – is a valid one. Recalling things you're grateful for works in the same way, by giving the mind good things on which to focus. It's a wonderful way to tap into the thoughts, emotions and sensations associated with things and people you love.

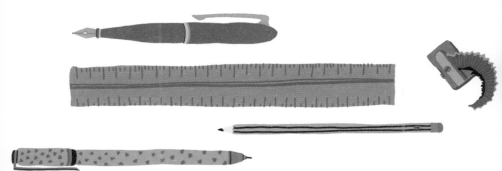

1 Take it slowly

Begin by taking a little time over the next few days to practise recalling things you're grateful for, without feeling the need to write them down. This will help you to become familiar with the activity.

Start small – thinking of just one thing could help to change the course of your day. Once you're comfortable with this you can consider recording these things. Taking the time to capture the objects of your gratitude helps you to connect with the positive emotions they stir and really embed them into your mind and body.

2 Make it enjoyable

Once you find your gratitude groove you can progress to writing a list on a daily basis, and by making this an enjoyable activity you're far more likely to keep it going. Perhaps use a pretty writing book and nicely coloured pens or pencils to write your list. It doesn't need to be anything expensive or elaborate, just something that you like.

Connect with the act of writing your list. Writing in the old-fashioned way – using a pen and paper – can help to avoid the digital distractions that are more likely to crop up if using your phone or tablet.

3 Keep it simple

Aim to write three things each day. Just before bed is a great time to do this because you're more likely to feel relaxed and less distracted. It's also a good way to go to bed happy – the perfect lead-up to a night of sweet dreams.

It's often the little things in life that mean a lot, so write whatever comes to mind without questioning whether it's important enough. Maybe you're grateful for your super-squishy pillow or some new, fluffy socks. Or perhaps it's something you've experienced, like a friendly cat that came to greet you on your walk to school that morning, or a song you listened to with friends.

4 It's personal

The great thing about this is that you don't even have to share your gratitude with anyone – unless you want to. You don't need to reveal your thoughts to experience the benefit of writing a gratitude list because this comes from the process of recalling and reflecting. It's easy to feel shy when saying 'thank you' to other people, which can make you less likely to do it, or to hold back. By making this a personal activity you're able to approach it safe in the knowledge that it will be for your eyes only. Try to let your inhibitions go and write from the heart.

5 Savour and reflect

Connect with the thoughts, feelings and emotions that arise when you think about these things and let them fill your mind. Take the time to appreciate them.

6 Don't worry about it

Be kind to yourself. Don't worry if you don't manage to write your list from time to time. This is a lighthearted and enjoyable activity, not another task to stress about. Perhaps you're busy with exams, or had a late night out with friends: as the saying goes 'life gets in the way' sometimes. You can easily pick up where you left off the next day – it really doesn't matter. This is about what works for you.

WHY IS IT IMPORTANT?

There are many things you can be grateful for in life, but it's really easy to get caught up in everyday dramas and lose sight of them.

Psychological research on practising gratitude found that writing down three things you feel grateful for – making a gratitude list – was the most effective practice when it came to having an impact on emotions (not to mention the easiest), which means you're more likely to stick with it.

Take a moment, close your eyes and think of something you're grateful for. Notice the feelings you experience. Perhaps you have a smile on your face already or a warm fuzzy feeling inside. Does it feel good? Imagine being able to feel those sensations easily every day. Certainly worth a try, right?

LET'S HEAR IT FOR FRIENDS

Good friends will make you laugh, support you, lift you up when you feel down, listen to your problems and are great fun to be with, so take a moment to celebrate those who light up your life

As the Irish proverb goes, a good friend is like a four-leaf clover – hard to find and lucky to have. They'll laugh with you, cry with you and join you on adventures. Friends made at school or college are there to enjoy exciting experiences, to share nerves about tests and exams and be there to support you through the highs and lows. Of course, friends come in different guises. Some will share your interests while others will have views you might find challenging. What's important is that you can count on them to be there when you need help and that you're happy to do the same for them.

FRIENDS BRING PRECIOUS GIFTS

A sense of security
It can sometimes feel like it's a big scary world out there, but friends give you the confidence to face new or difficult situations. Just having a good friend next to you is enough to keep the nerves at bay and leave you feeling calm and relaxed. Not sure how to behave when meeting someone for the first time, or what to say? The reassurance that a friend is by your side can give you the courage you need.

A source of information
Let's face it, parents, guardians and teachers might know a lot about life, but what do they know about YOUR life? You probably don't share all the details with them. Some friends, however, can read you like an open book. Then again, if you share all your news and innermost thoughts with each other that's hardly a surprise. Together you can discuss and debate and learn more about yourselves. Friends can offer valuable advice too, so make sure you try to listen to them.

Scientists agree
No one makes you laugh quite like your friends. They put you at ease and bring the best (and silliest) side out of you. Research has shown that friendships have a huge impact on wellbeing, proving what you probably knew all along – spending more time with friends is one of the secrets to happiness.

HOW TO CONNECT

1 Get involved
Building close friendships isn't always easy, but one of the best ways to meet people is through extracurricular activities. Join a club or group that focuses on an activity you enjoy and you're likely to find people who share similar interests. Having something in common is a great start for any relationship as it's easier to interact, learn what they think and connect more quickly.

2 Be approachable
You may not realise it, but body language is important when trying to meet new people. Avoiding eye contact and crossing your arms gives the impression you're closed off and not interested whereas a smile is an open door to a new friendship. Similarly, observe other people's body language. Do they lean towards you when you talk, nod their head in agreement with what you're saying? If so, they may be a potential new friend.

3 Start chatting
Good friendships can take time. You need to get to really know each other, build up trust and share experiences. If you feel a connection with a person you meet and want to engage in a conversation, you could begin by complimenting them. Saying something nice about what they're wearing or doing is a great icebreaker.

YOU'VE FOUND A TRUE FRIEND WHEN...

... you can talk about everything and anything

Being able to discuss everything, from celebrity crushes to a crisis of confidence, is a great stress relief as you can share your deepest secrets without the fear of being criticised or judged. Honesty and trust are key in this privileged relationship, so much so that if a best friend tells you those new trousers look daft on you, you won't be (that) offended. That's how much you respect their opinion.

...they're always there for you

A best friend is usually the first person you turn to when things are bad. Your problems are their problems and they support you like nobody else will. They even have the ability to make you laugh when times are tough. Best friends see you at your best and worst, and accept you the way you are.

HOW TO SURVIVE WHEN PEOPLE DON'T LIKE YOU

Most people like to be liked. Humans are highly sociable creatures who love connecting with others. Sadly, however, there will always be people in life who for one reason or another – or even for no reason – don't like someone, and you may end up on their list. For many, knowing a person dislikes them is upsetting. It feels like a rejection and can cause anxiety, stress or depression. But if you ever find yourself in this situation, there are things you can do. For a start, stop worrying and realise that while you can't control others and what they think, you can take charge of how you behave and react.

LEARN TO LIVE WITH DISLIKE

Being disliked can be a painful experience, but there are ways to cope:

1 Think about who's being mean
If someone's being mean to you it means that:
* they're mean
* you've done something mean
* you're overreacting

Take time to think through the situation. Did you do something wrong? If so, you can try to resolve the problem by apologising, talking to the person concerned or writing them a letter. This may not change their opinion of you, or they may need some time and space, but at least you've tried to make peace. If you did make a mistake, learn from it, but don't beat yourself up about it. After all, everyone makes mistakes.

2 Are they worth it?
If you haven't done anything wrong, consider how important this negative person is to you and how much you want to be their friend. One of the biggest lessons in life is that not everyone gets on – and this stands for all ages. There may be personality clashes or it could be the other person is unpleasant and not worth your effort. Quite often, when someone dislikes others for no reason, it's because of their own problems. Maybe they're envious or need someone to pick on. Don't let others bring you down because of their issues.

3 Remember who counts
Forget the person draining your energy and remember who you need to look after most – yourself. Consider all the lovely friends and family you do have. They're proof you're a good person. Just because one individual doesn't like you, it doesn't automatically make you someone terrible. It means that, for some reason, you're this person's target and you're probably one of many they dislike. Speak to your friends about the situation and they'll reassure you not to worry. It happens to everyone at some point and no doubt they'll want you to return the favour one day.

4 Break away

If someone's being hurtful or causing you stress, don't be afraid to remove them from your life where possible, whether it's via social media or in everyday life. It can be tempting to want to try to win them over, but if this isn't easy, it could lead to more anxiety for you. It may be difficult if you're in the same classes, but you can ask your teachers if they will discreetly move you away from the source of your angst. Don't be afraid to talk to your family about it, too, and ask for their support, especially if the person's behaviour escalates into bullying.

5 Do what makes you happy

It can be hard to get over painful feelings, but remember you're in control of how you deal with situations. Take time to be sad, but try to set yourself a time limit and then move on. Do things which make you feel better and will occupy your mind, such as seeing true friends, doing some exercise or going to the cinema. Perhaps join a group to meet more like-minded people. There are many other lovely potential new friends out there waiting to be introduced so focus on what matters – you and those who are closest to you.

6 Does it matter?

Some people will like you. Others will not. How does the person's judgment of you impact your life? If it's minimal, what can you do to let go of your need to be liked by this person? And, what can you do to stay calm and not return the dislike? The more you can come to accept others as who they are, to stop yourself from trying to change their opinion, the more you can get on with your own goals. Try to rise above the dislike by forgiving the person for not appreciating what you contribute and forgiving yourself for reacting with fear or anger. If you are doing the best you can with what you have, worrying if people like you or not is simply a waste of your time and your energy.

7 Final advice

The only people's opinions you should worry about belong to those dear to you. Dealing with people who don't like you for whatever reason can happen at any age – at school, college or the workplace. Some people will never change and you may never know what their problem is. As Taylor Swift sings: 'The haters gonna hate' and the best thing you can do is 'shake it off' and focus on enjoying your life.

FIND THE BRIGHT SIDE AFTER REJECTION

The sting of rejection comes to everyone, but the challenge is not to get too disheartened – better times are just around the corner

Whether it's being sidelined suddenly by a group of friends or being told you've not made the sports team, rejection hurts. It can be painful and embarrassing and leave you feeling insecure. But one thing is for sure – at some point, everyone experiences the harsh emotion of being rejected.

It could be being ignored by people you like or not being selected for a role. Rejection could come from not being offered a place after a college or job interview.

Wherever it comes from, rejection stings and some people can become so insecure about the possibility of it happening again that they end up avoiding many exciting opportunities, in an attempt to swerve that sense of hurt again. However, there are many ways to deal with those feelings and bounce back, so you can learn to accept rejection instead of living your life in fear of it.

1 Accept it hurts

Being rejected for whatever reason may cause real emotional pain so don't be afraid to express the feelings you experience and take time out to process events. Cry, shout and write down how you feel – anything you need to do to get those feelings out. It's helpful to give them a label when you write or talk about them. For example, 'I feel upset that…' These are your feelings and they're normal. Wallow in that hurt for a short while, as it will then be easier to move forward.

If you keep the feelings in, they'll slowly eat away at you and the situation will be harder to overcome. Set yourself a time limit to feel sorry for yourself, and then get ready to face the world again. Otherwise you could be wasting time that could be better used embracing exciting new opportunities and making new connections.

2 Talk it out

Share how you feel with a friend, family member or teacher who you know will be a good listener. Everyone will have experienced what you're feeling and once you've told someone else, you'll start to feel less hurt and they'll give you some comforting words and advice, too.

Other people can give you a different perspective and also make you see the reality of the situation and how what seems a big deal right now is not as important as you think. It's also good to put your feelings into words as acknowledging them can help you move on.

Think about the kind of advice you'd give someone in your situation. It may help you to realise there are other solutions and opportunities ahead. However, it might not be a good idea to talk about it on social media, especially if you're upset and angry. You might regret it in future when your perspective has shifted (as it inevitably will).

3 Look back and then move forward

When you're ready, consider what happened exactly and why it didn't work out. Was it something beyond your control? Was there anything you could have done differently or would do differently in the same situation? It may be it's just bad luck but it could also be you learn something from what has happened. The important thing is not to exaggerate your faults or look for reasons you weren't chosen or were left out.

It's easy to be very self-critical after being rejected, whatever the reasons, and you may find yourself saying things such as 'No one likes me' or 'I'm rubbish', but try to stick to the facts. Be kind to yourself, otherwise you'll develop a deeper fear of rejection, which in turn will mean you'll stop putting yourself in situations where you can be accepted and enjoy success.

4 It will sting but not for long

Rejection isn't always about not being made a sports captain or a prefect, or being dumped by someone you really liked. It could be that no one gets a joke you make, you were left off the invite list for a party or you simply feel ignored in a chat. It's part of life, so try not to be too hard on yourself. Instead, congratulate yourself for trying or taking a risk, especially if it made you feel uncomfortable.

In need of a quick confidence boost? Think of all the times you've enjoyed those giddy feelings of success in the past. You will triumph again and you'll probably appreciate it more after overcoming obstacles to achieve it.

5 Be philosophical

Often, rejection isn't a personal attack on you. The other person – or people – rejected you and the 'issue' is with them. Does it mean you're worthless and not a good person? No. The situation just hasn't worked out for you.

It may be useful to remember the sage advice 'everything happens for a reason': consider what positives you can get from this and look for ways to turn it into a valuable new learning experience. Can you develop a necessary skill that you might have otherwise been lacking? You can use rejection to improve an aspect of yourself. One opportunity may not have worked out, but something else will.

Think positively and become a stronger person from it. Have belief that this is part of your unique journey in life and better things will come for you. Yes, rejection can be a harsh reality check, but it can actually nudge you in a better direction for the long term.

6 Give yourself an 'internal' hug

A quick way to restore your confidence after rejection is to remember all of the amazing qualities you have. Why not take a moment now to jot some of them down?

CHANGE OF FRIENDS

Good friendship groups are one of the most important ingredients of wellbeing. Sadly, however, you may find that instead of making you happy, some friendships make you feel down. If you have friends who make you feel negatively about yourself, it may be time to move on

Is it time to change?
The biggest indication you need to rethink your social circle is if you consistently feel unhappy or drained after spending time with your friends. It could be that you don't agree with the things they say or do to others, or even to you. Maybe you feel they've changed and you don't have the same interests any more. Perhaps it's nothing your friends have done, but you've changed. Many people fall out at some point, it's not uncommon. But if you're always feeling down or that your friends are holding you back in some way, consider your next step. Jot down a list of the positives and less-than-helpful things about your friendship in a notebook and this might help you work out what is best for you.

Can it be fixed?

When thinking about whether you can do anything to mend the friendship, try remembering why you became friends in the first place. It could be you were in the same classes or primary school, or perhaps you went to the same after-school clubs. For one reason or another, you're part of this friendship and have had fun times in the past. Try to consider what's changed to make you feel the way you do. Is it something that can be fixed by talking to them? Is it that you still want to be friends but just not hang around together so much? Sometimes it can help to talk through the issues with an independent person – if your school has a counsellor or nurse, they might be able to help.

Cutting ties without causing upset

Accept it won't be easy moving away from a group of friends. Even if you've tried to resolve any problems or talk to them about how you feel, they might be annoyed, hurt and struggle to understand what's changed. But, ultimately, you have to do what's best for you – so accept it may be tricky. To minimise the upset, try speaking to the people in the group individually and explaining how you feel using 'I' statements, such as 'I feel unhappy about this…', instead of blaming people or criticising others.

Changing groups

Before you leap into finding new groups to hang around with, take some time to consider what you want from a friendship. If you've had difficulties with friends or groups, you might feel wary about new relationships. Instead, take time nurturing friendships you have with one or two close people to help you rebuild confidence. It's better to have a few close friends than a group of people you hang around with but don't have a close connection to.

Ways to make new friends

Look at what clubs and organisations are on offer at school or after school. Choose something you're interested in or have a particular passion about and you're more likely to find like-minded people. At lunch, ask if you can sit with people you find interesting. Ask them questions, add them on social media and arrange to go out. Building good friendships takes time but it's worth the effort.

The truth about friendships

There's an old saying that friends are 'for a reason, for a season or for a lifetime'. It's easy to think your current friends will be your friends forever but the truth is that as you change, it's inevitable that who you spend time with also changes.

Over the next few years, you'll start college or work, join new clubs and meet new people. Friends will come and go and you will make new friends many times as you go through life – this is natural. Just because some relationships were short-lived, it doesn't mean they didn't matter or you (or they) were a bad friend. It's part of life. Focus on being the kind of friend you'd like and treasure all the good ones.

Before deciding if you need to make a change, take a moment to write down all of the things that are great about your friend or friendship group, then make a note of the things that might have become less appealing. Does one list outbalance the other?

DON'T BE SORRY

Do you ever start sentences with 'sorry for bothering you...' or 'sorry, would you mind if...'? Perhaps you feel an urge to apologise for every little thing, even when it isn't necessary, whatever's happened isn't your fault and there's no remorse. Sorry, why do you do this?

Why so many apologies?

Most people are taught from an early age to be nice and polite, to think of others, to say sorry when they make a mistake and take responsibility. That's just learning to be a conscientious member of society. But when you're apologising because someone's bumped into you, for the clothes you're wearing or the food you're eating, it could be a sign you're worrying too much about what others think and placing their needs above your own. There's a downside to always putting others first – by deliberately accepting blame when it's not justified, or fearing that situations might become awkward if you rock the boat, there's a chance that your self-esteem will suffer.

When to apologise (or not)

Next time you find yourself saying the word sorry, stop and ask yourself if you really need to apologise: did you actually do anything wrong? Do you want to accept responsibility for whatever has happened? If you do, then that's fine. But if not, don't put yourself down. It will only give people the sense you've failed in some way, that you aren't living up to their (or your) expectations. Similarly, are you using sorry as an automatic response, a get-out card to avoid awkward situations? Try to avoid this temptation and instead, stand up straight and be assertive.

Turn apologies into gratitude

Switching from sorry to thank you is an easy way to turn a negative message into a positive one. If you arrive late for lunch with a friend, try saying: 'Thanks so much for waiting. I'm late because…'. If someone points out a mistake you've made, acknowledge it and add that you appreciate them mentioning it in a constructive way. This will make them feel more comfortable about the situation and boost your confidence at the same time.

APOLOGY ALTERNATIVES

1 When you need to ask a question
Rather than starting questions with: 'Sorry, I don't understand…' find an alternative. Maybe: 'Can you go through that again?' or 'Could you give me an example, please?'.

2 When you interrupt a conversation
Knowing when and how to interject is essential, so wait for a break in the conversation and then say: 'Could I just add to that…'.

3 When you need to get someone's attention
Are you trying to get past someone? 'Excuse me' generally does the trick. Almost bumped into someone? 'Ah – I didn't see you there, how are you?'

4 If you ever have to give bad news
The phrase 'I'm sorry to tell you…' can increase the feeling of negativity. Instead, calmly explain what has happened and then offer support or help to find solutions.

DON'T apologise for circumstances you can't control.

DO take responsibility for your actions if you've offended someone.

DON'T apologise for the way you look, think or feel.

MIGHTY MOTIVATORS

Working together with your friends can bring out the best in you all

Imagine it's a Sunday evening and you're doing your art homework or some last-minute revision – how are you feeling? Are you doing it just so you don't get into trouble at school, because your parents are nagging you, or are you doing it because you're motivated to do well in that subject and get a sense of satisfaction from producing work to the best of your ability?

It's normal for anyone working on solo projects to experience feelings of boredom, anxiety or a lack of enthusiasm. The good news is that within easy reach of you are secret aids that can help you to unleash your full potential and overcome any lingering negative feelings – your friends.

If you can share your experiences with your peers, and work collaboratively, the chances are you'll encourage them and work to the best of your ability.

How encouraging others and sharing ideas can lead to greater self-motivation…

1 Sharing helps
Learning and growing with friends allows you to share experiences and make more of your own potential than you might otherwise achieve if you studied alone. They can encourage you if you get stuck – and you can return the favour. In a similar way, you can exchange ideas and tips – a friend might be strong in one of your weaker subjects and vice versa. Also, knowing others share your concerns about a project or essay can release any stress or anxiety, while a friend's enthusiasm for a task can often prove to be infectious.

2 Use social media
Consider how to share your goals so others can support you and you can help them. You could consider setting up a group chat for exam revision facts or tips. Friends could then add to it or ask questions. It may be you share images on Instagram, which show your progress on a task, whether that's a painting, improving fitness, practising an instrument or developing a skill. Having friends comment, answer questions and offer words of motivation will provide a real boost.

3 Get together
If you're working on similar projects or ideas, meet up for a fun brain-storming hour or two, whether it's in a café, a park or at someone's house. It doesn't mean you're copying each other's ideas, but you can share, ask questions and develop your own thoughts and understanding of the issues. So, if you're revising, you can quiz each other, share resources and boost each other's learning. If you're working on a physical goal, such as yoga moves or reaching fitness targets, practising together can help you progress quicker. Everyone will be at different levels or stages, of course, but collaborative working can make things more fun.

THE COLOUR OF YOU

Discover how you can use colour to improve mood and outlook

Life is incredibly colourful, offering all manner of tones, shades and hues to brighten the day, but there's more to colour than meets the eye. Did you know that light, and the ability to decode it through the senses, is the reason you see colour?

The science of colour, known as chromatics, is fascinating but the psychology behind colour, especially in relation to how it affects emotions and outlook on life, is intriguing. In their book, *Colour Your Life*, Howard and Dorothy Sun explore how understanding colour can add a new dimension to your perception of your environment. This hasn't gone unnoticed in the business world where warm colours such as red, orange and yellow are used to create a sense of warmth (handy for keeping down the heating bills) while green is believed to spark creativity and increase productivity.

Put aside the debate as to whether or not white is a colour and you're still left with the perception that it represents modernity – bring to mind a certain technology giant? Choosing the right colour scheme matters.

Applied colour psychologist Karen Haller is a leading international authority in the field: 'Colour is this amazing phenomena that can influence how we think, feel and behave. When we see a colour we instantly feel its effect, whether we are consciously aware of it or not.'

Each colour has its own energetic wavelength and, on a subtle level, this can affect mood. By understanding these energetic qualities, you can choose colours to suit your needs and bring out the best of your personality.

Shades of mindfulness

Look around you. What are the dominant colours in your life? Have you inherited and grown up with them? Do you always choose the same shades for your clothes, room and accessories? Are you attracted to some colours and do you avoid others? What about your friends and family?

Being mindful about how certain colours make you feel and discovering which ones resonate with you can have a positive impact on your everyday life.

Devon-based artist Anita Nowinska, who is best known for her sensuous flower paintings, landscapes and images of nature, is convinced colour in art can enhance mood. 'Colour affects the way we feel so powerfully, it influences mood, atmosphere and wellbeing. They have a massive impact on feelings and emotions. They can lift and energise you or relax and soothe you.'

PAINT YOUR MOOD

If you can, set aside some time to paint and experiment with colour. Mix and blend different paints to achieve different shades and then consider how each colour makes you feel.

It might be that you have a favourite (the most often cited favourite around the world is blue, with brown being the least liked), but if you try to embrace the full spectrum, you can tap into the distinct energy of each colour (take a look at our chart) whenever you need it. Feeling you could do with a lift? Try pink. Want to relax? Go green. Whatever your mood, let colours help you on life's journey.

WHAT'S YOUR COLOUR?

RED

Passionate, bold, adventurous, confident, exuberant, successful, motivated, energetic and optimistic.

Red is stimulating and dynamic, but too much can be considered fiery and aggressive.

Add a touch of red to boost your confidence and shake off laziness.

ORANGE

Flamboyant, enthusiastic, determined, sociable, lively, instinctive, risk-taking and competitive.

Orange is warm, vibrant and uninhibited, but can also convey self-indulgence and insincerity.

Use orange to boost your enthusiasm and stimulate creative thinking.

BLUE

Creative, expressive, communicative, inspiring, truthful, composed, loyal and sensitive.

Blue is calming and encourages tranquillity, but can sometimes increase feelings of sadness or indifference.

Tune into blue when you need to feel peaceful and calm.

PURPLE

Spiritual, empathic, magical, imaginative, intuitive, regal, visionary and free-spirited.

Purple symbolises nobility, wisdom and luxury, but can sometimes be considered indulgent and pompous.

Meditate with purple to soothe mind and emotions.

SILVER

Artistic, inspiring, elegant, spiritual, intuitive and graceful.

Silver is feminine, imaginative and illuminating, but can also be moody.

Add a touch of silver to tune into your intuition more easily.

GOLD

Charismatic, successful, prosperous, generous and extravagant.

Gold is masculine, dynamic and eye-catching, but can also relate to anxiety, misery and egotism.

Add a touch of gold to inspire abundance and success.

YELLOW

Happy, active, humorous, independent, friendly, spontaneous and bright.

Yellow has a sunny, joyful disposition, but too much can over stimulate, irritate or even cause nausea and anxiety.

Add a touch of yellow to give you a lift when you're feeling down.

GREEN

Affectionate, kind, considerate, practical, nurturing, emotionally intelligent, gentle, loving, down-to-earth and nature-loving.

Green is a healing, safe and harmonious colour, but can make you feel complacent or laidback.

Use green to help you relax and rebalance.

PINK

Tender, loving, innocent, sweet, frivolous, gentle, calming and luxurious.

Pink is pretty and feminine, but overuse can convey fluffiness and irritation.

Add a little pink to perk you up after you've suffered a disappointment.

BROWN

Earthy, dependable, rooted, secure, reliable, conservative, wholesome and honest.

Brown is a grounding, sensible, autumnal colour, but can also be considered boring.

Use brown as an earthy contrast with muted yellow, orange or purple.

BLACK

Independent, strong-willed, serious, dignified, cool, sophisticated, intriguing, mysterious.

Black is formal and refined, but too much can be oppressive and pessimistic.

Use black sparingly or with other colours to add depth, elegance and mystery.

WHITE

Peaceful, tolerant, balanced, sensible, pure, wise, hopeful, angelic.

White represents purity, integrity and perfection, but can feel cold, empty and isolating.

Focus on white to bring peace and comfort. Use it to complement other colours.

BRACED AND CONFIDENT

It's pretty standard to have braces at some point – it could be for just a short while or more than a year. It's likely there are at least two friends in your class with them. But that doesn't stop it being a daunting experience, especially when they're first fitted. Here, a brace-wearing student suggests how to keep smiling through it all...

You might need braces for three months, nine months, a year, two years. Yes, it probably sounds like a really long time to have metal crammed around your teeth, but get through the first week of being a brace-wearer and soon you'll hardly notice them – the time will fly by.

The first two days to a week can be hard. Your teeth are adjusting to these strange additions and they might ache a little or sometimes a lot. Mouth ulcers can appear, too, but they disappear after a day or two. Your orthodontist might recommend wax to put on the brace, which stops it rubbing against the gum, and your GP will help if the pain gets too much. Be honest if you're asked to describe the level of discomfort, if any, you're experiencing.

Nerves are natural

As well as the physical aspects of wearing a brace, there are the nerves. Worry and anxiety rush around your head when you first get braces. Will they look bad? Will people call me names? Is everyone going to notice?

For me, the first people who were going to see my braces (apart from my parents) was everyone at school! I spent most of the day trying not to speak and closing my mouth, especially as the braces felt huge and noticeable. In fact, most people didn't spot them and, if they did, said they looked normal. My kind friends said they were great.

Try to be your usual self and as carefree as possible, which will make you feel – and appear – more confident.

Helpful tips and tricks to make life a bit easier

* Carry a pocket mirror, so when you're eating you can check if anything's become lodged in your braces.

* Drinking water helps food get unstuck from the braces – always carry a bottle with you.

* Smile normally. Trying to hide your teeth will only focus more attention on them.

THE PRACTICAL CONSIDERATIONS

Choose your food

If your mouth is painful and it's difficult to chew, try sticking to soft foods such as pasta, porridge and rice. Soft fruits such as bananas (ice cream is a must if you have a sweet tooth) are also good. Your orthodontist will probably give you a leaflet on which foods to eat and which not to, but otherwise…

Yes, please:
Soup, pasta, soft cakes, rice, chilli, blueberries, raspberries, meatballs, soft cooked chicken, tomatoes, mash, yoghurt, kiwis, cheese, tofu, eggs, beans, ice cream, brownies, peas and steamed veggies.

No, thanks:
Hard crisps, pizza crust, lollipops, toffees, hard-boiled sweets, apples (you could have them cut up into small pieces), chicken on the bone, baguettes, corn on the cob, coke, orange juice and sparkling water.

Choose your colour
It's exciting thinking about which shade of braces to get and there'll be a variety of colours to choose from. If you're struggling to settle on a favourite, here are a few things to bear in mind:

* Darker colours may make your teeth appear lighter.
* Lighter tones can make your teeth look more yellow.
* Choose shades that complement your eyes.
* You can always get more than one colour.

Choose who to talk to
Talking to friends, family and other students with braces can be helpful as it's reassuring to know they have had similar experiences and feelings. They'll also tend to be open to questions. And when the time comes, you can do the same for someone else.

Choose to distract yourself
Keeping busy doing things you love will help to take your mind off any pain and worries you have about the way you look. Go see a movie, spend time with close friends, read a book or jump on your bike, whatever makes you feel happy.

Choose to be you
At the end of it all, braces should make your teeth easier to clean – and clean teeth mean fewer fillings, and fewer fillings should mean you won't need implants (or even false teeth) later on. The thing to remember is you look great whether or not you have braces and to be confident about what you look like and who you are.

`USE YOUR SMILE TO CHANGE THE WORLD, BUT DON'T LET THE WORLD CHANGE YOUR SMILE'

ARE SELFIES MAKING YOU SAD?

Posting pictures of yourself on social media can be easy and fun. But sometimes it can also cause anxiety and insecurity. Here's how to steer clear of selfie–sadness

There was a time when no one would dare take photos of themselves for fear of looking too vain, or obsessed with themselves and their looks. But now everyone does it, and so often that it's even got its own word – selfie – and a place in the dictionary. Smartphones make it super easy and their nifty editing filters often produce funny and quirky results – many of which are promptly posted. But how many selfies are too many? Can you be addicted to taking them? And could they be affecting your confidence?

1 Copying Kim and Kylie

A whopping 17 million selfies are uploaded to social media every week in the UK. Many are posted by teenage girls, following in the footsteps of reality TV and red-carpet favourites Kim Kardashian and Kylie Jenner, who regularly share images of their 'perfect' pouting selves. For some, taking selfies becomes such a habit that they post to their Instagram stories or Snapchat from the moment they wake up to the time when their head hits the pillow.

2 Making a comparison

It's almost impossible not to compare yourself to the people who populate your social media feeds with their seemingly perfect pictures, but it's important to remember that people rarely post their true selves. Instead, they opt for heavy make-up and suggestive poses. Often, older people are trying to look younger while younger folk are trying to make out they're in their late teens or even 20s.

This is where airbrushing apps come in – removing spots, blemishes, freckles and scars; brightening skin, teeth and eyes; plumping up cheeks. Ultimately, they're disguising reality. Anyone can fake perfection with a filter on their face, so try not to compare yourself to their posts. And who's going to upload a picture where they're looking tired or red-eyed?

3 Addicted to attention

For some, posting selfies is a bit like a test to see how attractive people think they are. It's normal to want to receive reassurance, but it can lead to low self-esteem if you judge yourself by the number of likes and comments that are put up.

4 Ignore the haters

Putting your photo out for public approval will often attract positive comments – but there'll always be someone who's struggling with their own insecurities who'll post hurtful remarks, often anonymously. One cruel sentence can seriously dent a person's confidence, no matter how hard they try to ignore it.

5 Stay selfie safe

To ensure you're selfie safe, set your social media sites to private. It's also useful to know the people following you. Social media doesn't have to be a popularity contest, so don't be concerned by the number of likes you receive.

6 Avoid the addiction

Addiction is a strong word, but it's important to keep an eye on how many selfies you post and why you're doing it. Do you enjoy the feeling of getting likes? Do you post because you need a boost? Or are you posting because it's a genuinely nice photo, taken at a special event, that you wish to share? If posting selfies is more about seeking approval, it might be time to think about changing your selfie habit.

SELFIES – THE ALTERNATIVES

* Make your social media feed interesting in a different way by sharing photos of things you see and interesting scenes.

* If you feel brave, post images of the 'real' you, such as a make-up free image or just a natural shot rather than a posed or highly edited one. It might inspire your friends to do the same.

* If you're posting selfies because you feel low, boost your mood by doing some exercise, chatting to friends or doing an activity that relaxes you.

* Remember to try not to compare yourself to others based on the selfies they post – most are not true depictions of real life.

* Funny-face filters can be great, but limit their reach to close friends and family.

SCREEN SAVERS

Simplifying your relationship with the internet is easier
(and better for you) than you might think

Today's world is full of distractions, and with so many elements fighting for your attention, it's easy to feel overwhelmed. One of the biggest distractions is the internet – most people can't resist checking it throughout the day. After all, someone may have posted a cute cat video that you can't possibly miss!

The internet is a wonderful resource that allows people to keep in touch with family and friends from all over the world. But the downside is it can be addictive, meaning you may spend too much time online. Hours of screen time skipping and scrolling from one item to the next can make you feel restless. It may also affect your relationships, interrupt your sleep patterns and in some extreme cases make you feel unhappy about your life in comparison to others. Despite this, there are many benefits to being online and the web is a great place to find inspiration and connect with like-minded folk. It opens many doors and best of all the majority of information found online is free.

To help you achieve a better balance without the internet taking a hold of your life, it's wise to set some boundaries. This can be done by limiting your screen time and simplifying what you're consuming and engaging with. Think of it as 'the joy of missing out', because by switching off you can become fully present in your life and in this amazing world.

Over the page are four simple steps to a healthier relationship with the internet. If you try some or all of these tips you may notice a difference. Simplifying is a great way to ditch distractions and focus on your passions and what makes you truly happy. And by being fully present in your life you can enjoy the little things a whole lot more – a life focused on the present that is enriched with people, adventures, growth and creativity is a fulfilling one. After all, nothing on your phone is as important as the person or people sitting in front of you.

HOW TO MANAGE YOUR INTERNET TIME WISELY

1 Set some healthy boundaries
One of the most positive actions you can take is to set some boundaries. There are a few different ways to achieve this, from creating particular times you will be online, to not looking at the internet first thing in the morning or last thing at night. For example, you may wish to only use your technology between 9am and 7pm, which will enable you to enjoy a slower paced morning and fully unwind at the end of the day. It's easy to log on for a brief catch up and find you're still there an hour or so later. The internet thrives on keeping people distracted, so don't be too hard on yourself if you sometimes get swept away. Try setting an alarm on your phone to alert you when it's time to switch off and get back to the real world.

2 Reduce notifications
A great way to ease distractions is by removing the majority of notifications from your phone – after all, if someone needs you urgently you can be sure they will call. Silencing the flashing, bleeps, pop-ups and so on will stop you from being disturbed or being tempted to pick up your phone.

3 Simplify who you are following
If you've spent quite a bit of time online, by now you probably follow a number of different people, businesses, shops, organisations, etc. These numbers steadily grow, and before long your news feeds are full of things you no longer have any interest in. Every now and then it's worth spending a little time evaluating your lists. After all, do you need to follow a shop you have outgrown or an organisation you're no longer passionate about?

4 Spend some fun time offline
By taking an afternoon, day or even an entire weekend offline, you can fully focus on the people and the world around you. Spending time away from the hustle and bustle of the internet can enable you to fully engage with the simple things in life. A digital detox can also help you to look inward at what you want from life, because it's difficult to find your true path if you're drowning in online noise and activity. Time away from the internet can make you feel energised and better equipped to see the bigger picture. It serves as a great reminder that the real world is out there and worth your full attention.

#FUTURE
PROOF

How to protect your future
self on social media

So many people today are addicted to their phones – checking what's happening
on social media sites like Snapchat, Instagram, WhatsApp or Facebook,
commenting on a friend's new profile pic or their latest pair of trainers. It's
something older people don't always understand.

You've probably heard adults say that when they were young, they didn't spend so
much time looking at a screen. But your parents grew up without mobile phones
and in the 'olden days' of the 1970s, 80s and 90s, when you left school you often
didn't see friends until the next day. Usually you had to wait until after 6pm to call
anyone as that's when phone calls were cheaper. Remember, adults have lived in
a world with and without social media – and some of their concerns about what
you're posting could be worth thinking about.

With everything you post being saved somewhere in cyberspace – even when
you delete it – and with people missing out on jobs and college places because
of things they posted years ago, do you know for certain that what you're posting
is safe? Here's how to manage your social media accounts so you can protect
your future self.

YOUR DIGITAL FOOTPRINT

Every time you go online, you leave a trail – it's called a digital footprint. Like a real footprint, it means you leave a mark each and every time you use the internet to do things such as send an email, upload a photograph, download a video or comment on a forum, blog or post.

What difference will it make?

You might not worry about it now, but all kinds of people may look at your digital footprint in the future. It's quite common for colleges, universities and employers to look at the online profiles of possible candidates as part of the application process. Many people have lost out on places or jobs because of things they posted in the past.

In 2013, for example, Paris Brown was offered the role of Britain's first Youth Police and Crime Commissioner but had to turn it down after offensive tweets she made three years earlier, when she was 14, caused a media storm. Try searching for yourself online and see what comes up and remember others may be able to find things you can't.

SO WHAT IS SAFE?

Posting pictures or making comments is fine. The important thing is to think before you post – would I be happy with my gran reading this? Am I happy for this to be seen by anyone, now and in the future? Think carefully about the language you use or that joke you play or that photo you put up. Would you be happy for it to be online forever? Also think about how you could leave a positive digital footprint, such as writing a blog on the great things you are doing, a fundraising page for an event or a YouTube video teaching people how to do something.

Worried for a friend?
Most social media sites have the facility to report unwanted or abusive content or anything you're concerned about. On Instagram you can also report any friends you are worried about if they are posting images that make you concerned for them. You can do this by clicking on the three dots in the top right corner, tapping 'Report' and then selecting 'It's inappropriate – self injury.'

Private – keep out!
Your online reputation is valuable, but don't panic, no one is telling you to stop posting things. Just stay safe and be smart about how you use the internet and social media. The first thing you should do is check out the privacy settings. Most social media sites will have settings where you can control whether or not people can access your photographs, posts and comments. You can make your account private and approve any new friends and followers.

TOP TIPS
* Check your privacy settings.
* Don't post anything you wouldn't want your parents, teachers or future employers to see.
* Be yourself. Consider how you can leave a positive footprint.
* Don't share personal details like your email address or phone number, especially with people you don't know.
* Remember that while adults may think LOL means 'lots of love', they usually have your best interests at heart.

ARE YOU REALLY MISSING OUT?

Summer's here and the sun is out, so why are you feeling so down? Could it be a case of FOMO?

Summer holidays ought to be one of the loveliest and most relaxing times of the year, but some people find that this season can make them feel just as fed up as dark and gloomy winter. The reason? FOMO.

FOMO, an acronym of 'fear of missing out', may be a modern concept, but it's a real phenomenon – so much so that it has earned its place in the Oxford English Dictionary, where it's defined as: 'Anxiety that an exciting or interesting event may currently be happening elsewhere, often aroused by posts seen on social media.'

When the summer holiday sends you and your friends separate ways, it's understandable to feel slightly out of the loop. What makes it trickier is that you're able to stay up to date with what everyone's doing via messages and social media. Except that rather than making you feel more connected, this can end up causing you to feel anxious and left out. Is everyone else having a better time than you?

WISH YOU WERE THERE

1 Remember you're not alone

Recognising this feeling as normal – everybody, no matter how 'lucky' they appear, will occasionally feel like someone else is in a better place than they are – is the first step towards tackling it. So, you're having summer at home and one of your best friends is in the south of France. While you're envying her seemingly glamorous lifestyle and all of the experiences she's having without you, she's quite possibly yearning for the comfort and security of her own home and friends. Knowing that you're not alone in feeling what you're feeling can help you manage any worries.

2 Live the present moment

What else can you do? Take a step back and look at the good things about your current situation. Encourage your mind to shift its focus away from where else you could be and concentrate instead on where you are. How does the sand, or perhaps grass, feel under your feet? How does the fur of your cat feel to stroke after she's been lying in the sun? How does that ice cream taste? Remind yourself that you will never again have this exact moment, so make the most of it.

3 Look beneath the surface

Recognising the limitations of social media is another useful tool in tackling FOMO. When you're seeing photos of your friends having fun together, remind yourself that platforms like Instagram really are just a 'highlights package' – you're only seeing a few isolated incidents. Are your friends likely to post pictures of the times they're made to tidy their room, being bored at home or arguing with their parents about having phone-free time? Nope, probably not. Are they going to post about the multiple outfit changes, the sudden acne breakout and the sick, nervous feeling in their stomach before they go to the party that you're missing? No again. Remember that the 'advertised' bits of someone's life are not the only bits.

NO.1 APPOINTMENT:
YOU

If schoolwork, chores, sports and social groups are taking over your
life, it might be an idea to look at why you're so busy and clear a
space in the diary to make time for yourself

'Life's so busy.' That's something that you probably frequently hear adults saying, but actually, isn't your life pretty hectic, too? School will take up a good chunk of time, of course – and then there's study, homework, extra-curricular activities, sport, friends, family, chores…

Okay, deep breath.

The thing is, many people feel that they thrive on being busy. Not only does it give them a sense of fulfilment, but they also live in an age where they're encouraged to work hard and be their best selves. When you're brought up to mind your manners, saying no, especially to friends and family, can seem difficult, or even rude.

This can leave you feeling pulled in multiple directions. A parent may have organised a day for the two of you to spend some together. Meanwhile, your best friend is going through a tough time and wants your support. And then there's that Geography test coming up. In all of this, where are you, and how do you feel?

Unfortunately, taking on too many things can end up making you feel stressed. And this has its own negative effects – restlessness, irritability, lack of focus and sadness to name a few. Having space to take a breather is vital at any age, but especially when you're going through rapid developmental changes. Allowing yourself time to switch off properly gives both body and mind the chance to slow down, which is essential for wellbeing.

WRITE IT DOWN

List-making is one way to make sense of what's going on. When everything is feeling like a whirlwind of jumbled commitments and 'don't forgets', it can be helpful to set things out in a manageable way. Information that feels confusing in your head can often make far more sense on paper. Use a blank page to sketch out your commitments where you can see and observe them and you'll be better able to figure out which ones to prioritise and which ones to put back – this will leave some time for you.

Some things are largely non-negotiable. Homework has to be done, curfews need to be adhered to, hours of sleep need to reach adequate levels – if not always, then at least more often than not. When prioritising your activities, think about these factors. Friends are also important, but in most cases, they're torn between just as many obligations as you. Speak honestly to each other as this will lessen any guilt around putting them lower down on your list than, say, practice for an upcoming sports match, and also enable you to support one another in a practical way. For instance, you could look at ways to combine time together and your other commitments into a single activity – studying together for a test, for example.

'SMILE, BREATHE AND GO SLOWLY'

Thich Nhat Hanh

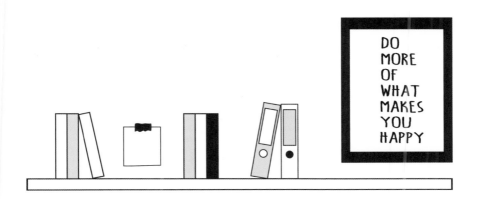

DO MORE OF WHAT MAKES YOU HAPPY

Need to? Or feel you ought to?

Often things feel like they can't be cancelled, postponed or put back to a later date. Guilt plays a large part in this. When you've made an arrangement with someone, you're reluctant to change it in case your actions are seen in a negative light. The other issue is boredom, which few people have positive feelings about, thinking it to be a bit wrong and a sign of ignoring all the wonderful opportunities they're always being told about.

There are two sides to this coin: often, when tired and over-committed, you may think 'I wish I could just do nothing'. Yet having nothing to do can create feelings of boredom and anxiety. So, consider those blank spaces in your schedule from a different angle. Change your perspective. When you choose to free up your time, those empty spaces can take on an entirely different flavour.

Empty spaces are full of ideas

Resetting thought processes around boredom can be an incredibly positive thing. Think about a new notebook. All of those completely unmarked, unlined pages – they just beckon the nib of your pen, don't they? How about a blank art canvas – what's more tempting than that first dab of the paintbrush?

If you can bring yourself to empty your schedule of all of those things that feature less predominantly on your list than others, you're allowing your mind some blank-canvas time, which will provide an opportunity for a much-needed reboot as well as a chance for free-thinking and creativity. All of which, in turn, can help you to be more able to handle everything you need to do in your busy life. You can make this work.

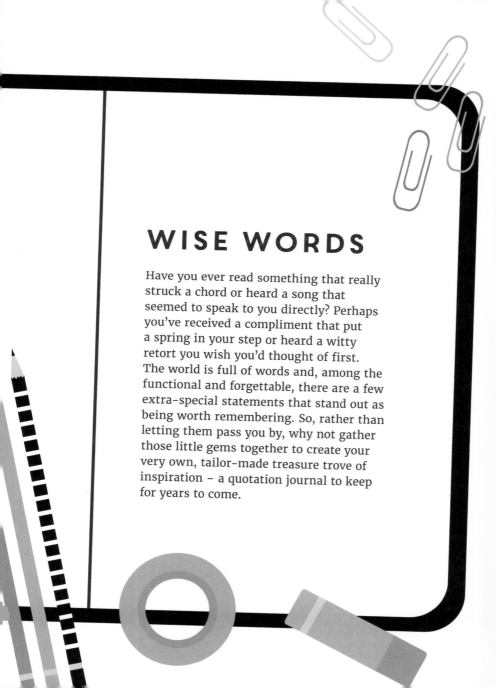

WISE WORDS

Have you ever read something that really struck a chord or heard a song that seemed to speak to you directly? Perhaps you've received a compliment that put a spring in your step or heard a witty retort you wish you'd thought of first. The world is full of words and, among the functional and forgettable, there are a few extra-special statements that stand out as being worth remembering. So, rather than letting them pass you by, why not gather those little gems together to create your very own, tailor-made treasure trove of inspiration – a quotation journal to keep for years to come.

WHAT DO I NEED TO DO?

Starting a quotation journal is simple. All you need is something to write with and a notebook. You could stick to a traditional jotter and a plain black pen, or pick a book that's more decorative and opt for glitter pens and coloured inks – whatever feels right for you. Paper does have an advantage in that it doesn't need to be compatible with anything else and never needs charging. Plus, your own handwriting will make the whole thing feel more personal. Once you have your stationery ready, it's a matter of keeping your eyes and ears open – then scribble down any quotes that have an impact on you, along with the name of the source and the date.

Try to keep subjects optimistic and upbeat – quotes should ideally make you feel happy, motivated and enlightened. Remember, though, this is a book entirely for your own enjoyment, so there are no rules really (unless you say so, of course).

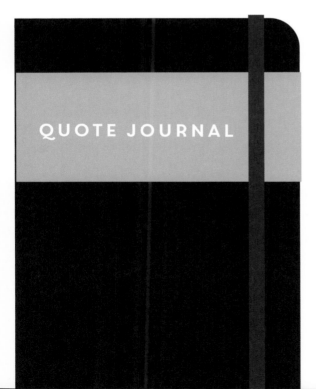

QUOTE JOURNAL

'Be original: don't be scared of being bold!'

Ed Sheeran

WHY CREATE A QUOTATION JOURNAL?

A quotation journal can serve many purposes:

* It's a fantastic way of keeping track of all those lovely snippets you might otherwise forget. If a quote made you smile when you first heard it or read it, it's likely to make you smile again in the future, and having a book full of those mood-boosting references to hand can prove invaluable over the years.

* It becomes a great resource to fall back on when you're looking for just the right words. You might be seeking a quote that helps to prove your point in your homework, searching for the perfect message to write in a greeting card or simply in need of encouragement to get you through a difficult patch. The fact someone else has experienced a similar situation and written or spoken about it can help – you can relate on a personal level.

* It can chart your own attitudes and values over time. Keeping track of the quotes that mean something to you at particular moments in your life can help to maintain a link between your former and current self. Looking over them can be illuminating and it may be something you'll cherish in years to come.

'Nothing is too wonderful to be true'

Michael Faraday

WHERE SHOULD I START?

Starting any new project can be daunting, especially if there's a beautiful, blank notebook involved – but don't delay! This is a project that will grow along with you and the sooner you start, the sooner you can reap the benefits. If you sit and wait for what seems the perfect quote before beginning, you'll never get going. Instead, choose something immediately – perhaps from a novel you're reading or a favourite song, or maybe you have a motto or mantra that would serve as a good opener.

Whatever you go for, once you have your first entry, set yourself a target. Perhaps aim to add one quote a month for the first six months and before long you'll find that gathering them will become second nature – and you'll start to notice snippets of wit and wisdom in unlikely places. On a practical level, don't worry about carrying your journal around with you all the time, there's no need. You can make a note of a meaningful quote on your phone or on some scrap paper, then enter it into your book at home later on.

Ready to go? Start creating your own positive, powerful and thought-provoking journal today.

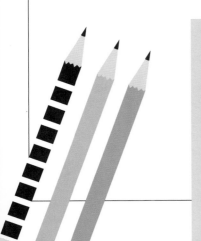

It's hard when you feel down and you think: "Why is the world doing this to me?" But you have to pick yourself up again. That's what makes you a better athlete'

Jessica Ennis-Hill

WORLDLY WISDOM

No one's born with the insight of learned philosophers, but give it time and it's possible to gain a deeper understanding of the world around you

From ancient Chinese teacher Confucius to 20th-century French philosopher Simone de Beauvoir, a look through the history books reveals a string of enlightened people whose insights have been amazing. But they weren't born with superior knowledge. This comes with openness and experience.

Life is a process of learning, of ups and downs. And if there's anything that helps to deal with its challenges, it's wisdom – the ability to make the right judgments and choices. But this only comes with time. You could consider life as a game: learning the rules gets you started, but the more you play, the more chances you have to win. It isn't always easy, but be courageous and go beyond self-doubts. If you learn from all of life's lessons – the good and the not-so-great – wisdom will follow.

THINK FIRST AND TALK SECOND

LIFE WILL PRESENT CHALLENGES – DON'T RUN AWAY FROM THEM, JUST DO THE BEST YOU CAN

LEARN TO RECOGNISE THAT NO ONE IS PERFECT

SLOW DOWN AND TAKE TIME TO OBSERVE THE WORLD AROUND YOU AND LEARN HOW IT WORKS

ACCEPT AND USE CONSTRUCTIVE CRITICISM IN A POSITIVE WAY

SEE YOURSELF AS YOU TRULY ARE – QUIRKS AND ALL

DON'T JUDGE OTHERS, ATTEMPT TO UNDERSTAND THEM

TRY NOT TO MAKE HASTY DECISIONS

WORDS TO THE WISE

hello friday

LOVE THE WEEKEND

When you arrive home on Friday after a busy week, the prospect of two free days to do whatever you want is exciting. Then Monday comes round again and you're left wondering what happened to your weekend. Sound familiar? Here's how to make the most of this valuable time...

WHAT'S STEALING YOUR PRECIOUS HOURS?

If weekends seem to pass in a daze and leave you feeling unfulfilled and deflated, then take a good look at what's taking up your time so that you can consciously make better choices…

SMILE *it's* - SATURDAY -

* **Gaming and television**. Are you gaming or watching television for hours and hours and feel like you're wasting your weekend? Limit your screen time and make room for other activities.

* **Sleeping later than usual**. It's nice to know you can have a few extra Zs at the weekend but if you spend too long in bed you're losing a big part of the day. Enjoy an occasional lie-in, but give yourself a good reason to wake up earlier.

* **Boredom and indecision**. Moping about because you don't know or can't decide what to do is frustrating. You can remedy this by thinking about what you'd love to do before the weekend arrives and then making firm plans.

* **Technology**. Constantly checking texts and social media to see how friends are enjoying their free time will eat into your weekend. You could consider putting your phone or computer away for a few hours or allow yourself to check in just once a day for 30 minutes. Focus on making your own weekend something wonderful to write about.

THE ART OF GOOD PLANNING

1 Decide what you'd like to do
To make sure those hours between Friday night and Monday morning are fulfilling, decide how you wish to spend your time. Is there something you'd like to learn or experience? What do you find interesting or entertaining? Where would you like to go? Do you prefer an action-packed weekend or something more relaxing or a bit of both? The hours are yours, so make sure you're doing what you love.

2 Keep a weekend diary
Use your diary, online calendar or a wallchart to create a weekend planner. Write down how you'll spend the morning, afternoon and evening for both days. You can track your weekend by the hour, but you don't have to follow it religiously nor schedule every moment. Set appointments for what you have to do (a Saturday job or family commitments) and what you'd love to do. Leave space for those magical moments.

3 Be prepared
Plan before the weekend arrives. Leaving it until the last moment can contribute to being indecisive and unorganised and more hours in bed thinking about what you might do with the days, which means you'll waste precious weekend time. Do some research (where needed). List what's required and then make any preparations early so that you're ready to go.

4 Make it doable
It's tempting to cram in lots of activities but trying to do too much to check things off a list isn't satisfying or even doable. You can end up feeling frustrated and disappointed. Instead, focus on quality rather than quantity. Aim to include between three and five things on your planner that you know you'll adore doing and that will make your weekend enjoyable.

5 Don't be predictable
Predictability can quickly become boring so rather than sticking to the same routine every weekend, mix things up. Try something new. Go somewhere different. Make new friends. Accept an invitation. Breaking routines occasionally will keep things fresh and avoid falling into a weekend rut. Of course, if you find something you absolutely love and don't want to miss it, always book time for that.

6 Take a breather

If you've created that diary or wallchart suggested in point 2, then think about scheduling in some downtime. It's great to have an action-packed weekend, but it's also essential to include space to relax and breathe. Go for a walk with a friend, read a book, listen to your favourite music or think about practising some yoga or a breathing exercise.

7 Leave room for the unexpected

Allow for spontaneity. You really don't have to plan every single moment: that would take all the joy out of your weekend. Be kind to yourself and create a looser schedule that supports you. Your weekend is there to enjoy not endure.

8 Think ahead

Be organised so you use your time efficiently. If you can, complete any non-essential chores on a weeknight. Plan for the following week on the Friday evening so you truly make the most of your Sunday. Keep as much of your weekend free for what you love.

LOVE Sunday ♡

True bliss

A LIE-IN

After a week of early starts, switch off your alarm and make
the most of that extra time in bed come Saturday morning

1   As you begin to feel yourself waking, make a conscious decision to
    keep your eyes closed. Lie on your back and become aware of your
    breathing. Try to keep it slow and relaxed, paying attention to how
    your chest rises and falls with each inhale and exhale.

2   Is your room warm or cold? Is there a breeze coming through an
    open window or is the air still? Notice the warmth (or chill) and
    how it feels on any parts of you outside the covers.

3   Listen to the beat of the house. Are any other family members
    already up and around?

4   Are there smells wafting up the stairwell and under your bedroom
    door? Is there a suggestion of coffee brewing or maybe a hint of
    bacon sizzling under the grill?

5   Think about what you might like to do for the day. Do you
    need to get up soon? Or maybe you have a free day?

6   Open your eyes and let the room come into focus. Is the
    sun coming through the gaps between your curtains?

7   Take a few more deep breaths. Savour this
    time before the weekend begins.

CALLING ALL DAREDEVILS

There are a wealth of organisations across the country that focus on introducing their young members to new skills and experiences so they grow in confidence and expertise. So what are you waiting for?

1 Teamwork and leadership

It's inevitable that you'll make new friends when you join a club or organisation, perhaps someone at a different school or from another culture. You'll also quickly feel very much part of a team, learning and having fun with others, all with the same interests. Understanding the importance of teamwork, and appreciating that everyone has an important role to play, will stand you in good stead throughout life. Teamwork teaches you how to listen, negotiate and compromise, all crucial interpersonal skills. And if you're given a role of responsibility, for example, being a Patrol Leader in the Scouts, you'll learn about leadership too.

2 Discovery

Whether it's how to sail or care for a dog or pony, youth organisations can help you to develop existing skills as well as open your eyes to new things to learn. Who knows, after a first-aid demonstration you may be inspired to pursue a medical career. It's not just the physical side of learning how to do a specific task either, such as lighting a campfire; when getting to grips with a new activity, you're also being taught to think critically, be resourceful and disciplined. These are all valuable attributes and will impress others when applying for work or future study.

3 Confidence and achievements

In a safe environment, where everyone gives encouragement and wills you to succeed, your confidence will quickly grow. Strong networks develop, and it's inspiring to watch others in your group achieve their goals, which spur you on to do the same. Got a fear of heights? When you've just abseiled in front of supportive friends, you'll feel like you can conquer anything.

4 Thrills

Although it's great learning about photography or how to grow vegetables, the more adventurous will want to hike outdoors, attend camps and participate in exciting exploits. Fortunately, many organisations give you the opportunity to do just that. Scouting, which is open to anyone between 10½ and 14 years, takes its members rock climbing, parascending and zorbing. Aged 14, you can also get involved in the Duke of Edinburgh scheme, and embark on an expedition.

5 A sense of identity

Members of clubs and organisations have a sense of belonging, and can enjoy spending time somewhere everyone is accepted for who they are. It doesn't matter if you struggle with maths homework or don't own the latest smartphone, you're accepted as a Cadet or Pioneer. And if you work with the community, such as the Young Farmers' Club, others in your area also benefit.

6 Happy days

Everyone needs a break from the usual school routine, homework and chores, and clubs and organisations are a great escape. What's more, research findings suggest that people who were in the Scouts or Guides are less likely to suffer from anxiety or mood disorders when they reach 50. That may seem like ages away to you now, but it proves that lessons in resilience and being active outdoors can have a lasting impact.

Pursue your
PASSION(S)

When you're passionate about something – surfing, cycling, dancing or whatever that might be – fun and rewards await

When you spend time doing something you truly love, whether that's baking delicious cakes, discovering more about the solar system or playing tennis, it's the best feeling in the world. Your energy and enthusiasm know no bounds and you appear invincible. That passion you have about photography, calligraphy, collecting all things elephant-related, whatever it is, will also encourage you to set goals, stay focused, make new friends, travel and much more.

DO WHAT YOU LOVE

So, what are you waiting for? Find something to be passionate about – anything – and start reaping the benefits…

1 You'll feel happier
There's nothing more rewarding than spending a few hours doing something that puts a big smile on your face. Whether you're running around an athletics track or cross-stitching birthday cards, that time spent concentrating on a hobby or interest you love will help you to focus and relax. Worried about a project you have to do at school? Indulging in a passion is a great way to unwind, and will help to put any feelings of stress or anxiety to the back of your mind, leaving you revitalised and ready to tackle anything.

2 You'll become more disciplined

Even if your passion involves hard work and doesn't come naturally, such as learning to play the violin or trying to stay upright on a paddleboard, having a passion encourages you to be more disciplined. It may be a challenge, but few people want to be just okay at a sport or craft they enjoy, or have an average knowledge of a subject that fascinates them. And as with all things, dedicate time and effort and you will see improvements – and that's a catalyst to continue. Who knows, you may go on to achieve great things.

3 You'll make like-minded friends

If you're passionate about ballet dancing, chess or musical theatre, chances are you will attend classes or clubs with people who have similar interests. New friends can also be made, though, if your passion involves doing something on your own. Say, for instance, you love mountain biking and often explore nearby tracks alone. If your passion motivates you to enter a competition, you could be introduced to others who love cycling, people attending local schools who you wouldn't normally meet. Social media networks can connect you too.

4 You'll discover new destinations

Having a passion about something can take you to amazing new places you'd not see otherwise. Love snowboarding? You could end up visiting idyllic ski resorts in the French Alps or Spanish Pyrenees. Imagine if this passion stayed with you throughout your lifetime – it could be the stimulus to book a holiday in the Canadian Rockies. Even delving into your family tree could prompt a trip to another part of the UK to meet distant relatives.

5 You'll widen your outlook

When you develop a passion about a topic or pastime, it's inevitable you'll learn more about other hobbies and subjects. A fondness for painting watercolours could ignite a desire to understand more about great artists, such as Albrecht Dürer and JMW Turner. Then an outing to a museum displaying their works could spark yet another love for a different art style. Before long, you could have a knowledge worthy of a place on *Mastermind*.

6 You'll make a good impression

Those individuals with a passion, and who can demonstrate it's helped them to develop, will have the edge over others when it comes to applying for a college or university place. Talking about your passion during an interview, and explaining what you've learned and how you've progressed, will impress recruitment teams. And your love for something may even be a route into a future career. Enjoy writing short stories or learning first aid? Stay focused and one day you could be the author of a best-selling novel or a researcher in medicine. Getting paid while enjoying your passion really is a dream come true.

'IF YOU DO WHAT YOU LOVE, YOU'LL NEVER WORK A DAY IN YOUR LIFE'

Marc Anthony

Keep
DANCING

Dancing isn't just about throwing great shapes on the dance floor to impress friends, it's one of the best forms of exercise there is for physical and mental health. It's also a creative way to get moving, can help improve fitness levels and co-ordination and practised regularly helps to maintain strong bones, improve posture and build muscle strength. Dancing also allows you to combine a full body workout with listening to good music. What's not to love?

1 Mind and body

Yes, your body can benefit from dance, but it's great for the mind too. Recently, there's been a lot of research into the benefits of dancing on mental health and the conclusion is that dance and movement have great psychological benefits, especially for people who experience depression.

Dance is a way of using the body to express emotion, which can be an advantage if you're someone who finds it hard to show your feelings. And it allows you to unwind as it gives you something specific to focus on when you're learning new steps and keeping in time to the music. When you're dancing you can forget whatever else is on your mind, particularly any worries you may have, and completely lose yourself in the melody and movement.

2 Feel positive

Dancing encourages the brain to release a flow of chemicals that improve mood and can leave you feeling positive and exhilarated. Practising on your own is fun and hugely beneficial to health but extra benefits can come from dancing as part of a group because it can make you feel more connected and sociable. Dance classes are a good way of developing your moves and people who learn to dance when they're young tend to carry on throughout their lives and benefit from being much fitter in later life.

3 Salsa, street or ballroom?

There are plenty of genres to choose from including ballet, tap, modern, street, jive, line, salsa and ballroom, so there's bound to be a style of dance that appeals to you. Most accredited dance schools hold beginners' courses and they're a great way to meet new friends even if you don't take to that particular style straight away. It's worth trying a few different classes until you find the one that's right for you.

4 Just go for it

Don't let worry that you won't be good enough put you off. Everyone worries they're not going to be good at something when they start out. You might think to yourself: 'Who's going to be there? I bet they'll all be better than me.' But the fact is everyone in that class will likely be feeling the same way you are. And if dancing with others isn't your thing, then why not experience the wonderful freedom and enjoyment of dance at home? Find a space where you feel relaxed and won't be disturbed, choose your soundtrack – some old favourites or upbeat pop tunes – and dance like no one's watching!

SPORT, PASSION AND THE ART OF NOT CARING

Turn negative experiences into positive opportunities and up your game

There's something freeing and invigorating about running around a sports field, diving into a swimming pool or chatting in the changing room with a bunch of people who have nothing in common besides a mutual love for one particular sport. It's a chance to forget everyday responsibilities for an hour or so and just enjoy yourself. It's a form of escapism.

Passion for a sport is a wonderful thing, and motivates people to do things they never dreamed possible. But it can sometimes result in a weird stalemate and what was meant to be an escape route can feel more like prison if you start to lose control of your mental game. Training sessions can become less about pushing your body and more about straining your mind worrying about skill progression, or lack thereof.

During team sports, the skillset of the individual doesn't matter. It's more about coming together as one and performing as a unit. A team is only as strong as its weakest link, and with that in mind, the pressure to improve and grow as an athlete can leave you feeling overwhelmed. No one likes to be left behind, but combine that with concerns or worries that you're letting down the team and you have a lot to handle. Thankfully, there are things that can be done to combat the negative mental strain, or at least to keep it at bay.

'YOU HAVE POWER OVER YOUR MIND, NOT OUTSIDE EVENTS. REALISE THIS, AND YOU WILL FIND STRENGTH'

Marcus Aurelius

STOICISM: THE ART OF NOT CARING

The idea of stoicism and its virtues can be useful when it comes to sorting out a negative headspace. Stoicism was first developed in around 300BC by a Greek physician, Zeno of Citium, and its philosophy comes down to four fundamental virtues: wisdom (approaching difficult situations with a logical and level head); temperance (exercising self-restraint); justice (treating others with fairness even when they've done wrong); and courage (facing challenges with integrity). In short, it's about learning to make the best of bad situations.

'Stoicism is the distinction between what you can control and what you can't,' says author Ryan Holiday in his popular 2014 book *The Obstacle Is The Way: The Timeless Art Of Turning Trials Into Triumph*. 'That's probably the hardest idea of professional sports – that you have to detach yourself from the results and focus exclusively on what you do and do it well. You can't get mad about missing the shot, or losing a game, or calls that went against you. You have to focus on what you were supposed to do and whether you did it right.'

The same applies to amateur sports. Instead of imagining ideal situations and environments, stoics focus on dealing with the world as it is. You may not be able to control outside variables, but you can determine how you react to adverse situations. You can't control what others think of you, but you can determine how you see yourself. Stoicism is the art of not caring.

That's not to say you should lose the passion – instead, channel it into something else, and view what you would usually consider negative experiences as positive opportunities. If you don't make the game roster, try to learn from those who did. If you don't beat your opponent, set new goals to up your own game. Just care less about the things you can't control and take comfort in the knowledge that there are some things you can't change. It's hard to enjoy a sport or hobby when you're worrying the whole time, and what's the point of having hobbies you can't enjoy?

OWN GOALS

Hopes and aspirations don't have to be long term –
you can improve your mental game on a weekly basis.
Here's how…

1 Set yourself reachable goals
Before each training session, note down three things you want to work on in regard to your own skills. If you succeed, celebrate your wins for that session. If you didn't quite reach your goals, think about why you didn't. Was something holding you back? Was it a lack of opportunity? Try to pinpoint a reason so you can improve next time.

2 Track your progress
Attempt to quash any doubt by thinking about your skill level before you took up the sport, and compare it to where you are now. The difference can be immense. Then start thinking about how much progress you can make in a week, and where you would like to be in seven days' time.

3 Involve a friend
Talk to a teammate about your goals before every session, and what you both want to achieve that day. When you're no longer alone in tracking your progress, goals become less of a burden and more of an exciting challenge. Also, you'll have someone else watching out for your wins.

4 And remember...
The first and foremost reason to participate in sports is to have fun! Try to enjoy the sport for what it is and don't allow winning to be a condition for enjoyment. Anything worth achieving is rarely easy – practice, practice and still more practice is required to master any sport. Learn to see a competitive situation as an exciting challenge rather than a threat, and you'll be achieving something worthwhile.

RUNNING FREE

You don't have to run as far and as fast as Mo Farah to call yourself a runner. All you need to do is put on your trainers and start moving to enjoy the many benefits the sport has to offer. Not only will it help keep you physically fit, it will also sharpen your mind, improve your skin and boost your mood. What's even better is... it's free!

Here are a few reasons why running could be the new hobby for you…

1 It will make you feel fit

Everyone knows the more exercise you do, the fitter you get, and running is one of the best ways to work your whole body because it tones your legs, arms and core muscles. Running also reduces the risk of chronic illnesses like heart disease and type 2 diabetes. If that's not enough to get your trainers on, consider how running improves your posture, which is really important after all those hours sitting hunched over a desk in class and lugging your heavy school bags around.

2 It will make you feel fabulous

You'll always have something to congratulate yourself for when you start running. While the first run might feel hard, the second run will feel easier and you will notice improvements each time, whether it is running further, faster, stronger or just getting less out of breath. You'll feel a real sense of accomplishment every time you return from your run and will quickly find you've got the 'running bug' and look forward to your sessions. You'll also notice you find everyday things, like going up the stairs or even walking to school, easier and that your body tones more quickly. When you feel good physically, you feel good mentally too.

3 It will release stress

As well as the running bug, get ready for the running 'high' which occurs during and after your running. Each sweat session produces a surge of feelgood chemicals – endorphins – that make you feel happy and ready to tackle the world. Running reduces the body's stress hormones so it's the perfect way to clear your head after a hard day or get ready for something ahead. If you're preparing for exams or making decisions or just busy, it gives you excellent thinking time and space. In fact, a survey by mental health charity Mind found that 94 per cent of respondents said exercising outdoors in nature improved their mental health.

4 It's something you can do alone – or in a group

While you can get involved in team sports at school or college or join clubs that are local to home, running is something that can be enjoyed on your own without the worry of feeling self-conscious and have others criticising you. It's just you competing against yourself and your last time or distance. You can listen to music and just focus on yourself. If you think you'd prefer running with others, you can get involved with a running club, charity run or one of the 5km parkruns, which will give you a means to compete while also improving your running ability.

WHAT DO YOU NEED TO GET STARTED?

SHOES. The most important thing you need are some good running shoes which will give you the support and cushioning according to your feet and your running style. If you can, go to a running shop where they will analyse your 'gait' (how your foot falls) and recommend the right kind of trainers to get the most out of your runs and stay injury free.

BRA. Another really important item to invest in is a decent sports bra as your chest will need proper support. You can buy sports bras in most shops that sell bras – just make sure yours is suited to high-impact activities.

COMFORTABLE CLOTHING. Look out for technical or 'wicking' clothing (this moves sweat away from the skin) and socks and comfortable sportswear that won't rub, cause you to overheat or create blisters.

WATER. It's important to keep hydrated so ensure you take a bottle of water with you. You don't need to worry about any fancy sports gels at this stage, but do make sure you've eaten something an hour or so before you run.

GO SLOW

The best way to start is slowly. Use a mix of walking and running, starting with mainly walking, otherwise you'll get despondent, bored and ache a lot. There are plenty of apps and websites with great ideas to get you to your first 5km, such as the 'Couch to 5k' app. You can also find apps to track your run: these show where you've been, how fast you've gone and how far. Some of the most popular are 'Map My Run' or 'Nike+ Run Club'.

The main thing is to take it slow and steady, include lots of walk breaks, keep your head up, shoulders and hands relaxed and breathe deeply and rhythmically. Don't overdo it – but don't give up too easily either. You'll find you'll get out of breath at first and may get a stitch but try to schedule in three sessions a week and within a few weeks you'll realise you're improving quickly and may even start thinking of entering a parkrun near you: parkrun.org.uk.

STAY SAFE

If you're running alone, it's important you look after yourself by following these tips:

* Run in public areas that you are familiar with.

* Always tell someone your running route and take your phone with you.

* If you can, avoid running with music on or with it too loud. You need to be aware of the traffic around you and not distracted from any dangers nearby.

* If you're running when it's getting dark, wear a headlamp and brightly coloured clothing so that motorists can see you.

* Hydrate. It's important to take a drink with you.

World of
BEAUTY

From flowers to puddles, beauty can be found almost anywhere.
All you need to do is learn how to look

For centuries, philosophers have been trying to understand what beauty means. Some say it's a subjective quality, that it's 'in the eye of the beholder'. So, what you find beautiful might not appeal to a friend.

Others think beauty is objective – in other words, that an object, like a painting, would always be beautiful, regardless of whether two people disagree over it.

Neither side of the argument seems closer to uncovering the truth, but one thing they agree on is this: experiencing beauty makes you happy. When you look at something you find beautiful, whether that's a puppy or a new pair of jeans, you usually feel some kind of amazement, awe or joy.

Beauty can, of course, come in all shapes and forms. You might find it in the bright, blossoming flowers in a garden, or in a horse majestically galloping across a field. It can be in music or poetry or the smell of freshly baked bread. You might find it in acts of kindness, like returning a lost item, or acts of rebellion, like standing up for a cause you believe in. What's important to remember is that it's your own experience, and only you know what you find beautiful.

If you can keep an open mind, you can start to find beauty in almost everything. Author AA Milne, who created the *Winnie-the-Pooh* stories, summed this up perfectly: 'Weeds are flowers too, once you get to know them.'

It's a statement worth keeping in mind as it captures the notion that even the things normally thought of as ugly or undesirable, like weeds, can be viewed differently if you give them a chance – if you give them the attention they deserve.

BEAUTY IN THE EVERYDAY

To help you get started, below are five techniques that will gradually help you open your eyes, mind and heart to the beauty in your life. Once you can do that, you'll start to notice how beautiful the world really is – even if you're just looking among the weeds…

1 Deliberately look

The ancient philosopher Confucius once said: 'Everything has beauty but not everyone sees it.' When you're outside, try to take a mental note of all the lovely things around you. Is the sun creating intricate shadows on the ground or nearby buildings? Can you hear running water or a bird singing? Look for it in the unusual. Perhaps the muddy puddles have curious reflections in them. Maybe you can see green shoots growing through cracks in the pavement or paint peeling delicately from the walls. If you make an effort to notice five beautiful things every day, over time it will become habit and you won't even have to remind yourself any more.

2 Put away technology

It's tempting when you're on your own to put your headphones on or pull out your mobile phone and check for updates. But scientific experiments have found that just having your phone near you – even when you aren't using it – can cause a distraction. When you're absent-minded, you aren't able to enjoy beautiful things fully, which can make you less appreciative of them. So, the next time you're walking home from school or sitting on the bus, try to put your phone and headphones away for at least five minutes and use the time to look around you.

3 Enjoy the slow life

Getting from A to B, whether it's school, footie practice or coding club, can take forever when you have to rely on public transport, lifts from family or your own feet. But when you're going slowly, you have the chance to notice what you wouldn't have spotted if you were zipping past. Perhaps you'll observe a squirrel in a tree or see a snail clinging to a leaf. The more time you spend outside, the more you'll see – and the more you'll likely appreciate.

'WEEDS ARE FLOWERS
TOO, ONCE YOU GET
TO KNOW THEM'

AA Milne

4 Talk to your friends or family about it

While beauty is a personal experience, it's also good to share your feelings. It might feel awkward at first, but try starting a conversation with your friends about what they think is beautiful. It can be eye-opening to hear other people's opinions. Don't forget that everyone is entitled to their own thoughts, though, so try not to make judgments.

5 Remember that beauty isn't just a physical quality

If you look hard enough, you'll start to see beauty in the abstract as well as the physical. Think about how beautiful it is that today you can speak to almost anyone in the world, no matter how far away they live or how long it's been since you've last spoken – and you can do it in just a few seconds. Think about that feeling of excitement you experience the night before a holiday or that lurching sensation you get when you drive over a big bump. Think about two people hugging at a train station when saying goodbye, or someone sincerely apologising for a mistake. When you start noticing beauty in even the smallest of actions, you'll quickly realise how beautiful life truly is – and how lucky you are to be a part of it.

HAPPY WHEN IT RAINS

Don't let those thunderclouds dampen your mood. People may moan about the rain, but it's time to change your perspective

It's easy to understand why some people complain or feel down when it starts to rain. Those brooding, dark clouds overhead have the potential to dampen the mood of even the most cheery of souls. Then, when the rain arrives – producing anything from a fine drizzle or sharp shower to a seemingly endless monsoon-type downpour – it can spoil plans for making the most of being outdoors. Wet hair, muddy shoes and being soaked to the skin – none of this sounds like much fun. Yet there's something truly beautiful about the rain and if you start to look at it differently, you might begin to appreciate it and, perhaps, even love a rainy day. Now, where are those wellies and an umbrella?

When it rains, there's nothing you can do about it – so you might as well make the most of the weather. You can learn to love everything about a rainy day by shifting your perspective and changing your outlook.

The author John Updike once said that 'rain is grace; rain is the sky descending to the earth; without rain, there would be no life'. How true. Rather than focusing on gloomy thoughts about the damp weather, marvel at its many benefits and beauty.

Watch how rain falls, creating pools and streams on the ground. Enjoy listening to the pitter-patter, splash or torrent of water. Notice how fresh everywhere around you looks after a good downpour. If you find yourself caught out in a shower, enjoy the sensation of raindrops on your skin. Jump in the puddles that have formed. Smell the rain-freshened air. Realise that despite the inconvenience of getting drenched, being outside in the rain can be invigorating and you'll soon dry off when you're back indoors.

You might even learn to love the rain so much that you'll be one of the special group of people known as pluviophiles. Finding joy and peace of mind during rainy days, a pluviophile relishes being outdoors in a shower without an umbrella and they look up at grey skies to welcome those first raindrops.

RAINY DAYS ARE GOOD BECAUSE...

1 If you've no plans to go anywhere, there's suddenly a wonderful opportunity to snuggle up indoors with a hot beverage while reading a book or watching a favourite film. This can be a perfect time for some essential pampering, writing in your journal or catching up on all the tasks you've been putting off for a while.

2 It can be enjoyable and refreshing to be outdoors in the rain. In warmer months, walking while it's raining can bring welcome coolness. During colder times, going outside dressed in wellies and waterproofs can be exhilarating, making you feel more alive.

3 Listening to the sound of rain as it falls can be relaxing, calming and comforting. Take a nap or close your eyes to meditate. This is a wonderful time to drift away and dream.

4 Rain is, of course, a crucial part of the cycle of life. It replenishes the earth, helping plants, flowers and trees to grow. A deluge of rain fills the rivers and reservoirs, providing essential water to live and thrive.

5 With a little imagination, those raindrops can be seen as full of mystery and magical qualities. Let them spark your ingenuity and inspire creativity. Some amazing original ideas can arrive during a rain storm.

6 Everything looks fresh, clean and sparkly afterwards. Have you noticed the pleasant, earthy scent that is produced when rain falls on soil or pavements? This is called petrichor and is especially noticeable immediately after a shower following a long period of dry weather.

MY RAINY DAY RECORD

The next time it rains, pause for a while and take notice. There are many types of rainfall to enjoy: drizzle, mizzle (fine rain that forms a mist), sharp showers, a spit, a deluge, thundery showers and torrential rain that goes on for hours. Listen to the beat and rhythm of the rain as it falls. Watch the shape and movement of raindrops on windows. See how the water creates puddles, gullies and spray. Go out and feel the rain on your face. Splash your feet in puddles. Do a rain dance. Be grateful for the beauty and life-giving properties of water, and then why not put down on paper – in words or pictures – what you noticed and how it made you feel.

NORDIC KNOW-HOW

When the going gets chilly, Nordic countries light up dark days with cosy, fireside gatherings crackling with friends, food and fun. Follow these hot tips from cold climates to help you thrive through the winter

When winter blows a gale and darkness falls at 4pm, you might feel a little hard done by, but spare a thought for those living close to the Arctic Circle – in midwinter there are only a few hours of daylight in the Nordic countries and, even then, the greyness can make it feel like dusk.

The Nordic region includes Denmark, Norway, Sweden, Finland and Iceland, and their associated territories – Greenland, the Faroe Islands and the Åland Islands. The long winter nights are caused by the tilt of the Earth, which spins at an angle as it revolves around the sun. During the winter, the northernmost parts of the Arctic Circle remain 'hidden' from the sun for 24 hours, so it is dark both day and night.

You might be surprised to learn that despite the long hours of darkness and plummeting temperatures, Norway topped the United Nation's World Happiness rankings for 2017, closely followed by Denmark and Iceland. So, just what is it that keeps these countries smiling all year round?

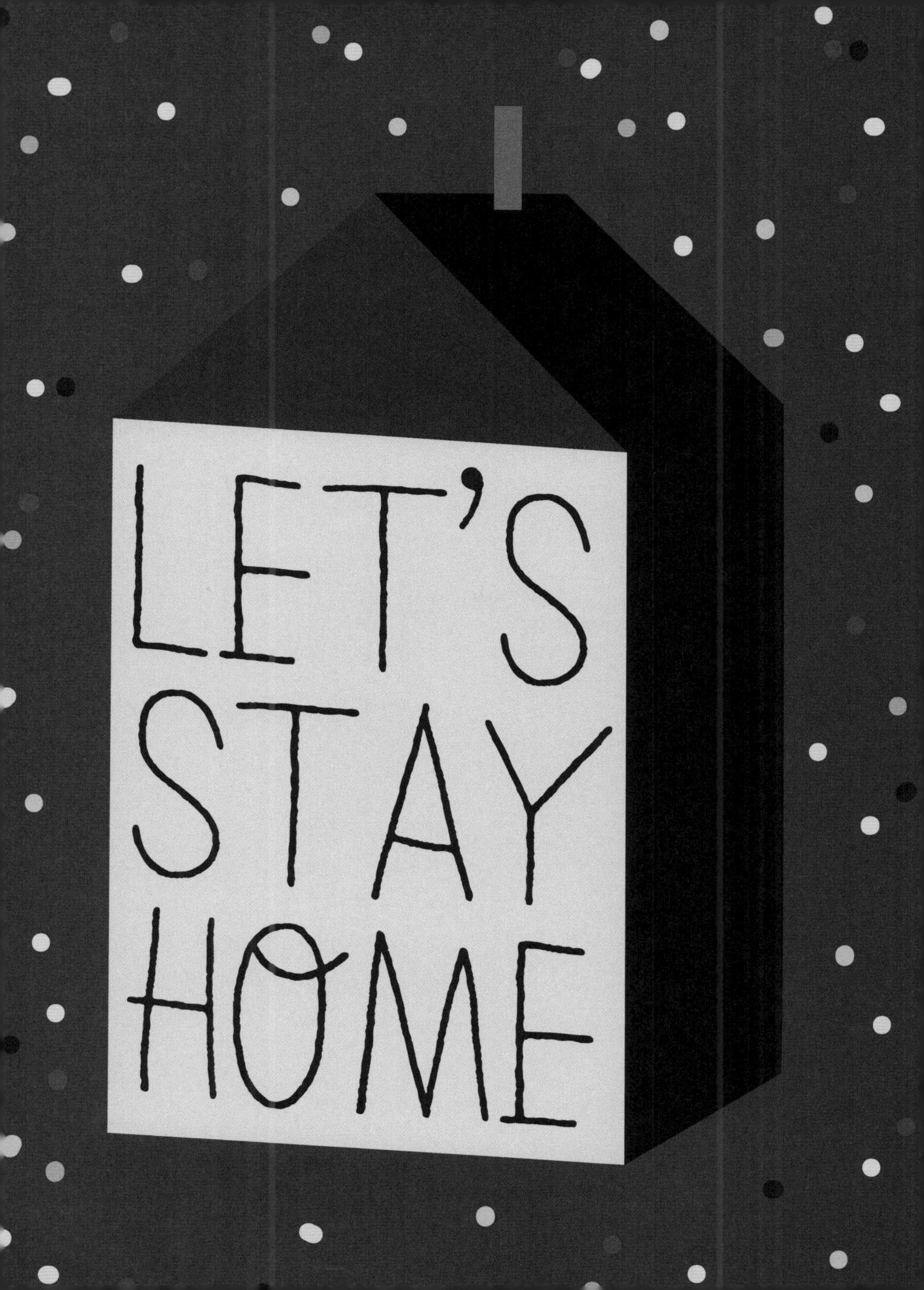
LET'S
STAY
HOME

Time for
HYGGE

> `PEOPLE DON'T NOTICE WHETHER IT'S WINTER OR SUMMER WHEN THEY'RE HAPPY'

Anton Chekhov

KOSELIG: HOW NORWEGIANS GET HAPPY

Koselig is a Norwegian word that means a sense of cosiness. It can be applied to anything that makes you feel happy and content. During the dark, cold, winter months, people gather to light fires and candles, and to enjoy hot drinks, delicious food and the company of friends and family. Snuggling under woolly blankets, they settle into cosy mode, focusing on the warmth and light that sets winter aglow. Koselig isn't just an excuse to sit on the sofa, veg out and watch Netflix though. There is a strong community aspect that inspires festivals and events that bring people together to chat and get active. The Swedes call this community energy livslust – a lust for life.

In Denmark, the word hygge describes a similar feeling – the wonderful sense of enjoying something and being completely enveloped in the experience – rather like getting a big, warm hug. Taking time to appreciate hygge is vital to happiness, particularly during the winter, whether it's enjoying the company of friends around an open fire, observing the stars twinkling in the night sky, or just watching a raindrop slowly trace its way down a window pane. It has been suggested that these positive ways of experiencing the world might help to explain why Nordic countries score so highly in happiness rankings.

NORDIC TIPS FOR SURVIVING AND THRIVING THROUGH WINTER

1 Layer up and get outside whatever the weather

There's a saying in Sweden, *Det finns inget dåligt väder, bara dåliga kläder*, which means there's no such thing as bad weather, only bad clothing. In the UK, people often bond over the dismal weather, but in Nordic countries the elements are something to be enjoyed rather than endured. Layer up Nordic style and get outside in search of fun whatever the weather. Wear a thin layer next to your skin – wool is ideal as it retains heat even if it gets wet. Add another thicker woollen mid-layer and a waterproof coat on top.

2 Change your mindset

Nordic countries embrace their winter and focus on the wonder and joy of the season rather than the darkness and gloom. The wind, rain and snow are a source of inspiration for poems, songs and artwork, and dark days are a time for creative reflection and a celebration of light, love and warmth.

3 Eat well

The Nordic diet is among the healthiest in the world, providing plenty of protein, omega-3s and antioxidants which support health and wellbeing. There is less emphasis on ready meals and fast food, with simple dishes usually being made from scratch. Fish such as herring, trout, mackerel and salmon are popular so try to get lots of oily fish in your diet. You'll be pleased to know that cinnamon buns and gooey chocolate cake are also a popular treat.

HOST YOUR OWN COSY KOSELIG GATHERING

Plan a koselig evening with family or friends. Crank up the cosiness with naturally scented candles, fairy lights, fluffy blankets and hot drinks. Ask your guests to wear winter jumpers and to bring slippers or woolly socks to snuggle up in. You could play winter-inspired music, too – it's all about firing up the conversation and serving some treats. And don't forget to blow out the candles before you go to bed.

Try these conversation starters for a cosy night in…

* What inspires you about winter? Is there a song or poem that brings the season to mind? Do you have a favourite winter memory?

* What could you do to bring more koselig and hygge into your life? And how could you help friends, family and pets to feel this, too?

* Take inspiration from Nanna, Norse goddess of the moon, who was said to bring joy and peace. Which values would you embody?

* Collaborate with your guests to tell winter tales that bring fire, joy and light into the season.

ANIMAL MAGIC

Your feathered and furry friends can teach you a lot
about dealing with stress

If you're a pet owner, you might have noticed that your faithful friend seems to find the pursuit of happiness and wellbeing a lot easier than humans do. Cats and dogs have shorter lifespans than people, yet they often seem so content and acutely alive. Even some animals in the wild, that face all kinds of challenges to survive, can literally shake off stress like water off a duck's back.

What can you learn from the many animals, large and small, that pass through your lives every day – some of which you may not even have noticed?

Instinct and intuition

Although your dog may at times look as if it's meditating, its behaviours are based primarily on instinct, whereas people are capable of more complex thought processes. Humans are able to reason and reflect, not only on their own lives, but on the universe around them, and their place within it.

One of the downsides of more complex thinking, however, is that people tend to worry about the past and the future in a way that animals don't. Constantly tuned in to your chattering mind, you can also lose touch with your gut feelings and intuition.

SHAKE IT OFF

Rather than suppress strong emotions as humans sometimes do, animals often shake off stress immediately after having a fight, flight or freeze response to danger. You might have seen this behaviour on TV wildlife programmes, when an animal such as an antelope has been pursued by a predator.

Instead of carrying pent-up stress around with you, try this simple animal-inspired exercise:

Begin by standing with your feet firmly on the ground. Shake your arms and hands and then each leg in turn. Gently bounce up and down and shake your whole body for a minute or so. Imagine shaking off anything that has been bothering you today. Finish by standing still – take some deep breaths and enjoy a moment of stillness.

Living in the here and now

Animals are great at living in the present and dealing with each moment as it arises, with focused attention. They accept themselves, understanding and adapting to their limitations – you won't find your cat losing sleep, racked with anxiety over something it did last week, or has to do next Tuesday. Of course, animals can become stressed if they experience long-term distress in the wild, or are mistreated in captivity. It's up to people, as custodians of the planet, to act mindfully to support their wellbeing, so that as far as possible their moments are happy ones.

Work, rest and play

Instinctively, animals know how to strike an optimum balance between work, rest and play – they listen to their instincts and act accordingly. Notice how most animals tend to focus on one task at a time with precision and patience, rather than multi-tasking like people do. They get plenty of rest (some even hibernate for an entire season) but when they do set about a task – finding food, making a nest or looking after their young – they focus on it 100 per cent, without distraction. Even though your dog or cat may appear to be sleeping much of the time, when they are tracking a scent or on the prowl they are completely in the moment, focused on the job at hand, with no thoughts of yesterday or tomorrow.

How do you decide when to work, rest and play, and what could you learn from your pet about your pace of life?

HOW TO PRACTISE MINDFULNESS WITH ANIMALS

* Become more aware of the animals you encounter as you go about your day – from the tap of a dog's paws on the pavement to a bird singing, or even a snail moving slowly across your path. Use their presence as mindfulness cues to stop and pay attention to what's happening in the moment.

* As you observe an animal (or conjure up the image of one in your head) notice the feelings you associate with it – perhaps affection, awe, fear or even irritation. All creatures contribute to the planet's ecosystem – is it possible to value an animal's contribution and feel gratitude towards it, whatever reaction it triggers in you? (This can be quite a challenge with wasps and mosquitoes!)

* If you have a pet, sit and just be with them. See if you can focus on their presence for a few minutes without getting carried away by other thoughts. Is there anything about them that you hadn't noticed before? Perhaps a detail in the pattern or colour of their fur, for instance. If appropriate, gently stroke your pet – notice how they react, and pay attention to how they feel to touch; become aware of their heartbeat and watch the rise and fall of their abdomen as they breathe.

A NEW, IMPROVED YOU!

Some view the new school year with dread while others relish the prospect. Either way, it's good to reflect on what went well over the past three terms and what you could do better

Like New Year's Day, the first day of the school year is an exciting time when you should feel anything is possible. With your brain feeling refreshed after the long summer break it can be a time for a new, improved you. Here's how to make some small changes for a big difference…

1 Reflect on the past

Look back at the previous year and consider what went well for you and what would have made things even better. Are there lessons you feel you could work harder in? Do you pay enough attention in class? Is your work always done to the best of your ability? Perhaps use a piece of paper or card to note down your targets for the next year in a positive, assertive way, such as 'I will hand all homework in on time' and pin it somewhere you'll see regularly. Speak to your teachers or counsellors at school and let them know you're trying to improve in a certain area and ask for advice. They'll be happy to help.

2 Check yourself

Are there any behaviours you think you could improve on? For example, do you worry too much? Or would you like to feel less shy? If so, now's the time to make changes to overcome these things. Try to do things that take you out of your comfort zone. Set targets such as putting your hand up more in lessons or vowing to stop worrying so much what others think. You'll be amazed how the more you do it, the easier it will become.

3 Treats galore

There's nothing like buying some amazing stationery, clothes or having a new haircut to give you a boost and make it feel like a proper fresh start. Go to your favourite stationers and treat yourself to some new pens and equipment, because the more you like them, the more likely you'll enjoy using them in classes and on homework. Why not get a diary or set one up on your phone to write down important dates and things to remember, so you are super organised?

4 Be open to new people

Part of going to school is about dealing with friendship and relationship issues. If you're lucky, you'll have friends who will always stick with you – but don't be afraid to make new ones too. It's okay to move in different directions and sometimes it's a positive thing, especially if you feel you've grown apart. New people help bring out other aspects of yourself and will teach you new things.

5 Join teams and clubs

Use the new school year to join clubs or sports teams you're interested in. School offers opportunities to learn skills and develop talents so ensure you make the most of them. You may even discover a hidden gift. It can feel nerve-racking at first, but try to remember everyone else will have felt the same when they started.

6 Don't give up

If you had a bad year last year, whether it was grades, arguments or friendship issues, resolve that this is a new beginning. You can choose how you react to others and what you want to do and think. Keep persevering and who knows, it might be the best year yet.

MY PERSONAL TARGETS

It could be handing your homework in on time, getting up 10 minutes earlier so that you're not rushing around in the morning, trying to go to the cinema more often or allowing yourself half an hour's quiet reflection at the weekend. Try to think of one or two things that you'd like to work towards.

WRITE A LETTER TO YOUR FUTURE SELF

Imagining what you will be like in five or 10 years' time and sending that 'you' a letter can be a fun way to think about your hopes for the future

Ever wished you could travel through time? This creative exercise is all about packaging up the present and offering it as a gift to your future self in years to come. By reflecting on what matters most to you now and on your goals for the future, you can be your own time-travelling life coach. How are you feeling about your life right now? What would you change and why? What do you want to say to your future self, and what are you hoping to have learned by the time you open this letter in five, 10 or 20 years from now? Collect your thoughts, then find a piece of pretty paper and have fun writing them down using these tips...

Packaging up the present

You could begin by addressing your future self as you would a close friend whom you haven't seen for a long while: ask how they are – what have they been up to? Explain that you are writing this letter to offer encouragement and inspiration.

Write about your life now: how old are you, what is a typical day like and where do you live? What are you grateful for? Consider the people and activities that bring you joy, and comment on your interests, talents and beliefs. What are you proud of? What is the biggest obstacle you have overcome in your life so far and how did it feel to make a breakthrough? Who do you admire and respect, and why? Also reflect on your fears and concerns, both personal and global. What would you like to change about yourself and the world around you?

Framing your future

Remember that life can be a rollercoaster of twists and turns, and it may be that on letter-opening day your future self is heading into a bend. Write down any words of encouragement you could offer. Think about your strengths and positive qualities now and remind your future self about drawing on these to stay strong.

SEND AND RECEIVE

* Decide on the age you want to be when you open the letter, then choose a significant date. This will help you remember to open it.

* Use 'I' when writing about your current self and address your future self as 'you'. You could include a photo of yourself, along with a poem or song lyrics that inspire you.

* Once you have finished your letter, put it in an envelope, seal it and write the following on the front: Your name. A letter to my future self, not to be opened until… {*insert chosen age and date*}.

Put the letter somewhere safe. Remember – it's for your future self's eyes only!

TEEN Breathe

TEEN BREATHE is a trademark of Guild of Master Craftsman Publications Ltd

First published 2019 by Ammonite Press
an imprint of Guild of Master Craftsman Publications Ltd
Castle Place, 166 High Street, Lewes, East Sussex, BN7 1XU, United Kingdom

www.ammonitepress.com
www.teenbreathe.co.uk

Editorial: Susie Duff, Catherine Kielthy, Jane Roe
Publisher: Jonathan Grogan

Words credits: Jenny Cockle, Lorna Cowan, Donna Findlay, Anne Guillot, Catherine Kielthy,
Olivia Lee, Kate Orson, Poppy-Jay Palmer, Victoria Pickett, Iris Prentice, Sarah Rodrigues,
Simone Scott, Carol Anne Strange, Gabrielle Treanor, Sally Turner

Illustrations: Shutterstock.com, Lucy Banaji, Anieszka Banks, Matt Chinworth,
Trina Dalziel, Katerina Gorelik, Stephanie Hofmann, Maria Mangiapane, Silvia Stecher,
Sara Thielker, Céleste Wallaert, Sarah Wilkins

Cover illustration: Charly Clements

ISBN 978 1 78145 476 3

The publishers can accept no legal responsibility for any consequences arising from the
application of information, advice or instructions given in this publication

A catalogue record for this book is available from the British Library

Colour reproduction by GMC Reprographics
Printed and bound in Turkey

AMMONITE
PRESS